ICELANDIC-CANADIAN MEMORY LORE

Magnús Einarsson

**Canadian Centre for Folk Culture Studies
Mercury Series Paper No. 64**

Canadian Museum of Civilization

© Canadian Museum of Civilization 1992

Canadian Cataloguing in Publication Data

Einarsson, Magnús

Icelandic-Canadian memory lore

(Mercury series, ISSN 0316-1854)
(Paper / Canadian Centre for Folk Culture Studies, ISSN 0316-1897; no. 64)
Includes an abstract in French.
ISBN 0-660-14004-7

1. Icelandic Canadians — Folklore.
2. Folklore — Iceland.
I. Canadian Museum of Civilization.
II. Canadian Centre for Folk Culture Studies.
III. Title.
IV. Series.
V. Series: Paper (Canadian Centre for Folk Culture Studies); no. 64.

GR113.7.I3E46   1992   398.2'094'912'0971
C92-099691-4

Printed and bound in Canada

Published by
Canadian Museum of Civilization
100 Laurier Street
P.O. Box 3100, Station B
Hull, Quebec
J8X 4H2

Printing Coordinator: Lise Rochefort
Cover Design: Francine Boucher

Canada

OBJECT OF THE MERCURY SERIES

The Mercury Series is designed to permit the rapid dissemination of information pertaining to the disciplines in which the Canadian Museum of Civilization is active. Considered an important reference by the scientific community, the Mercury Series comprises over three hundred specialized publications on Canada's history and prehistory.

Because of its specialized audience, the series consists largely of monographs published in the language of the author.

In the interest of making information available quickly, normal production procedures have been abbreviated. As a result, grammatical and typographical errors may occur. Your indulgence is requested.

Titles in the Mercury Series can be obtained by writing to:

> Mail Order Services
> Publishing Division
> Canadian Museum of Civilization
> 100 Laurier Street
> P.O. Box 3100, Station B
> Hull, Quebec
> J8X 4H2

BUT DE LA COLLECTION MERCURE

La collection Mercure vise à diffuser rapidement le résultat de travaux dans les disciplines qui relèvent des sphères d'activités du Musée canadien des civilisations. Considérée comme un apport important dans la communauté scientifique, la collection Mercure présente plus de trois cents publications spécialisées portant sur l'héritage canadien préhistorique et historique.

Comme la collection s'adresse à un public spécialisé celle-ci est constituée essentiellement de monographies publiées dans la langue des auteurs.

Pour assurer la prompte distribution des exemplaires imprimés, les étapes de l'édition ont été abrégées. En conséquence, certaines coquilles ou fautes de grammaire peuvent subsister : c'est pourquoi nous réclamons votre indulgence.

Vous pouvez vous procurer la liste des titres parus dans la collection Mercure en écrivant au :

> Service des commandes postales
> Division de l'édition
> Musée canadien des civilisations
> 100, rue Laurier
> C.P. 3100, succursale B
> Hull (Québec)
> J8X 4H2

ABSTRACT

This selection of 332 examples of Icelandic traditional poetry and other bound language contains children's rhymes, rigmaroles, riddles, lullabies and prayer verses, as well as adult lore such as dance and drinking songs, religious and humorous poems, plus proverbs and sayings. These texts are from a collection recorded in western Canada and two of the American border states, North Dakota and Washington, in the late 1960s.

RÉSUMÉ

Ce volume présente un choix de 332 pièces de poésie traditionnelle et de formes d'expression de la langue islandaise. Les comptines, les énumérations, les énigmes, les berceuses et les prières rimées y côtoient des pièces du folklore des adultes telles que les chansons à boire et à danser, les poèmes humoristiques et religieux, ainsi que les proverbes et les dictons. Ces textes sont tirés d'une collection de documents enregistrés à la fin des années 60 dans l'ouest du Canada et dans deux États américains limitrophes, le Dakota du Nord et Washington.

ACKNOWLEDGEMENTS

I wish to express my thanks to C.C.F.C.S. ethnomusicologist Dr. Carmelle Bégin for her musical transcriptions; to Heather Hucul for making this material presentable for publication; to my supervisors, Drs. Stephen Inglis and Paul Carpentier, for their support and encouragement; and to my friends and colleagues, Dr. Robert Klymasz and M. Lucien Ouellet, for their advice and assistance. And, as always, I wish to express my deepest gratitude to my many friends and countrymen in the Icelandic-Canadian communities who gave so generously of their knowledge and hospitality.

ICELANDIC–CANADIAN MEMORY LORE

TABLE OF CONTENTS

Abstract III
Acknowledgements V
Table of Contents VII
Introductory Note 9
Transcription Symbols 15
Rhymes About Familiar Animals and Pets
    (1-12) 19
Rigmaroles
    (13-30) 33
Nonsense Rhymes
    (31-48) 77
Riddles
    (49-82) 99
Game Verses
    (83-86) 137
Rhymes About Grýla and Other Scary Figures
    (87-99) 143
Lullabies and Soothers
    (100-105) 163
Prayer Verses
    (106-112) 171
Drinking Songs
    (113-119) 181
Dances and Reels
    (120-130) 191
Humour and Satire
    (131-135) 207

Narrative Poems
   (136-140) 215
Mock Narratives
   (141-142) 241
Proverbs and Sayings
   (143-332) 245
Music Transcriptions (Carmelle Bégin, Ph. D.) 299
Notes 319
Key to Abbreviations in Notes 349
Index of Tale Types 353
List of Informants and Their Contributions 357
Map 359

INTRODUCTORY NOTE

This volume contains a selection of traditional Icelandic poetry and proverbs collected during the second half of the 1960s in the Icelandic communities of western Canada and two of the American border states, North Dakota and Washington.

Much of this material is what in the English speaking world would be regarded as nursery lore, while the remainder is adult entertainment, religious and wisdom lore. I am calling all of this material, regardless of age-group affiliation, 'memory lore' because it has ceased to have much life outside of individual memory.[1] There are, of course, exceptions. A mother or, more likely, a grandmother will recite and try to teach a child a rhyme or a prayer verse if the primary language in the home is still Icelandic. And, at occasional gatherings where conviviality is enjoyed in robust measure, a song may still be heard in praise of women, wine and noble steeds. Likewise, proverbs may occasionally find their way into conversation. However, this type of formal Old Country lore, so dependant upon the language skills of performer and audience, and so readily replaceable with English language entertainment lore (oral as well as printed), increasingly falls on deaf ears among my informants' younger compatriots. What was once a shared experience is becoming more and more an individual memory experience.

Other reasons have been offered in my hearing for the decline of traditional lore in oral circulation in the Icelandic communities. Modern child-rearing theories discouraged the frightening or misleading of children with Old Wives' tales, and progressive members of the community frowned on the open display of this kind of "old-fashioned" peasant lore for fear of incurring mainstream ridicule. Also, and perhaps more importantly, women very likely had less time in North America to pass formally bound, and sometimes long and difficult, texts on to their children, at least during the early homesteading period. Life in Iceland, the argument goes, had been hard, but working life was set into predictable rhythms with established rest periods

---

[1] Folktales and other international entertainment narratives included in the first volume of this series, ICELANDIC-CANADIAN ORAL NARRATIVES (Hull, Quebec; Canadian Museum of Civilization, 1991) also fall under the rubric of memory lore, and for the same reasons.

that allowed for the sharing and teaching of folklore as well as other more important matters. There is probably much truth in all of this, but what must also be considered to be a critical factor is that many family elders, who normally would have taken up the slack as teachers, had chosen to remain in the Old Country, leaving their children's Canadian-born offspring without ready access to this type of lore, thus hastening its demise by a generation. Then, on the other side of the coin, the immigrants' children, and especially their grandchildren, became less and less receptive to this lore as language skills declined and Icelandic came to be increasingly spoken and understood as a foreign language. While words continued to be understood, their metaphorical tenor relating to history and culture, and especially values and feelings, became increasingly obscure and ceased to be able to enchant in the same way that similar English language materials now could.

Still, it can be argued that memory lore has had an important role to play. For my informants, whether born in Iceland or Canada, it has been a source of emotional comfort and readily available private entertainment that they can return to at will. One informant told me he recited rhymes and verses while doing monotonous farm chores, and another, having lost much of her vision, recited rigmaroles to pass the time when she was no longer able to read.

Also, at a community level, this material, along with other surviving Old Country artifacts and mentifacts, has taken on a certain symbolic value. Although most of the middle-aged and younger Icelandic-Canadians I met on my collecting trips didn't know this lore, many knew of it and knew people who knew some of the texts. The attitude of this younger set of informants toward this material was ambivalent, showing touches of embarrassment and patronizing amusement but also affection and respect. What seems to happen with mentifacts, as it does so obviously with artifacts, is that once they become separate from their original function and meaning, they are reinvented as souvenirs of a bygone age, and especially as icons or markers of ethnic identity. While this is indeed not as obvious with mentifacts as with artifacts I have interviewed enough informants to know that similar attitudes exist toward both kinds of materials. The text as objectified fact and vehicle of sentiment becomes more important than the text as a vehicle of entertainment and meaning.

The importance of this material for me as a folklorist is that it is an integral part of the overall Icelandic-Canadian folklore complex and it can't be left out of a representative collection. It is, of course, also instructive to look at this material and compare it with what exists in similar collections gathered in Iceland, to see what has been retained and what has been abandoned, and why. (This is a study that must be put on hold for another day, but, in general, the other great change in Icelandic-Canadian folklore, aside from symbolization, has been simplification, meaning that shorter and simpler texts have had a better chance of surviving the immigrant experience. This will become more apparent in my third volume dealing with occasional poetry. A third type of change, much apparent in the first volume of narratives[2], involves an emphasis on realism and an interest in individual experience rather than that which is fictional and non-specific.) On a more applied level, I see this material having value as a part of a resource package for anyone interested in Icelandic and Icelandic-Canadian language and culture. My special hope, however, is that this collection, recorded as it is from Icelandic-Canadian sources will be of use to young Icelandic-Canadians interested in exploring their own ancestral culture.

The texts in this volume fall basically into three parts. The first part consists of children's rhymes and riddles. The second part consists of adult entertainment and religious lore, and the third part consists of proverbs which should also be considered as adult lore. I have left out many items that I know or suspect to have been memorized directly from books but left in other items that, while they existed in print during the informant's upbringing, were, nevertheless, learned from oral sources. That also goes for the dance songs (nos. 120-130) which almost certainly first saw the light of day in print in pamphlets or magazines (many translated from Danish) but were quickly memorized and passed into oral circulation among the youngsters in the turn-of-the-century fishing villages of Iceland. This type of popular lore was so obviously an integral part of the repertoire of people who emigrated in the period between 1900 and 1914 that I felt it had to be included. This material reflects the big change that was then well under way in Iceland; namely, the move from country to seaside village.

My original intention was for this volume to contain only nursery lore, but it soon became obvious that my term 'memory lore' had a broader scope. Satirical and humorous poems, drinking verses, prayers, religious poems, and dance songs had to be included as well; that is, not just the lore of childhood, but also the lore of later years. To place all of this material under this rubric is risky. All of it has existed in oral circulation in Canada, at least for the immigrant generation and its children and, occasionally, its grandchildren. However, by the time I came upon the scene as a collector in the mid-1960s, it was largely confined to memory. One might describe the state of the rest of Icelandic-Canadian folklore at that time in a similar fashion, but with the difference that the verses and anecdotes and other reality-based lore was still being shared within a given age group. The memory lore, on the other hand, was only very occasionally being passed 'down' to grandchildren, and laterally among peers, almost certainly, never. People might still be interested in hearing and even learning a clever lampoon or a ghost story from a friend or a neighbor, but no one would bother passing along or learning a rigmarole or a folktale, unless specifically asked by those of us with a strong antiquarian interest.

A few words about my informants. Most of them are known from my previous volume (cited above) in this series. The large majority, 31 out of 43, were born in Iceland. Of these, slightly more than half (17) were from the north of the country.

---

[2] Op. cit.

were born in the eastern part, four in the southwest, and three in the northwest. Only one came from the inland agricultural region of the south. Most were children and teenagers when they arrived. Five of them were 5 years of age or under; four were between 5 and 10; five were between 10 and 15; and another five were between 15 and 20. Eight, however, were between 20 and 30; two were between 30 and 40; and only one was over 50 when she arrived from the southern quarter of the island.

The near-even gender spread was somewhat surprising. Only slightly more than half, or 23 out of 43, of my informants were women while 17 were men. I expected, for no very good reason, that there would be a much higher percentage of women informants. Specifically, I did not expect to find any men reciting rigmaroles. This is, generally speaking, a woman's genre but obviously not exclusively so. On the other hand, I had not expected to find women reciting or singing drinking songs, but this, in fact, turned out to be less uncommon than men reciting rigmaroles.

The numerical distribution of items I classify as memory lore was as expected. 37 informants recorded 10 or fewer items. Three informants recorded between 10 and 21 items. One informant, Mr. Valdimar Johnson, recorded 56 items, while Mr. Gunnlaugur Holm recorded 144 separate items, most of them proverbs. These two informants, as well as Mrs. Sigurveig Sveinsson, differed from the other informants, not only in terms of the number of items contributed but also in the nature of their interest. All of them, especially Mr. Holm and Mr. Johnson, made a special effort, in their spare time, to collect rhymes, riddles and proverbs. Mr. Johnson kept a notebook with the texts he had recorded, and Mr. Holm had also written down, and even alphabetized, his proverb collection. However, both men were very clear about what was their own personal repertoire, and what was learned from other recent sources. The texts I acquired from Mrs. Sveinsson came to me via a long, informative letter after our initial encounter.

One final statistical note: over half of my informants, 23 of them, were from the New Iceland region of Manitoba (along the southwestern shore of Lake Winnipeg), the home of the greatest concentration of Icelandic speakers in North America. Three other informants were residents of Winnipeg and southern Manitoba, plus one from near Lundar, also in Manitoba. Six informants resided in the Lake Settlements of Saskatchewan, an area just south of the Quill Lakes. Five informants lived in Vancouver; two resided in Blaine, Washington; and three in Pembina County in North Dakota.

The informants of this type of traditional lore were, of course, all of different background and outlook, but they shared certain characteristics. They were, by and large, people whom neighbors would refer to as being "good Icelanders" (= góðir Íslendingar). All of them spoke good Icelandic and made a point of staying in touch with Iceland and all things Icelandic. Many had been back to Iceland on one or more occasions, mostly on charter flights that began in the early 1950s.

Introductory Note

While the value of these "good Icelanders" as bearers of the Old Country culture has been invaluable, their knowledge is now largely unshareable, and their role, like so many other Old Country facets of ethnic life, has become symbolic. With their passing, in fact, one can see the demise of an active Icelandic culture in North America. Fortunately, however, that is not, of course, the end of the story, since the culture of the immigrant generation and their children has given rise to a uniquely Icelandic-Canadian culture. This 'new' cultural complex which has been gradually replacing the old, almost from the beginning, is reliant on the Old Country culture for most of its symbols and rituals of identity, and that includes texts such as the ones included in this volume. Whether they exist only in the minds of "good Icelanders" or in print, sitting on a parlour shelf, they retain their value, along with an array of other markers and identity icons, as symbols of this new culture—Canadian in content and intent, and Icelandic in look and form. On a qualitative, personal level, however, the greatest value of these texts lies in the pleasure and comfort they give to the few who are still able to enjoy them not merely as symbols or souvenirs but as vehicles of imaginative transport.

A few words about the translation. I tried where I could to translate line by line, rather than verse by verse, and I tried to have each line retain its original word order. I tried, likewise, since I see this as documentary resource material, to avoid being overly artistic. I sincerely hope, however, that someone will, in fact, volunteer their service in making these texts artistically more appealing for a general readership.

Hull, Quebec, 1992

WORK CITED

Einarsson, Magnús. 1991. ICELANDIC-CANADIAN ORAL NARRATIVES. Mercury Series, Paper No. 63, Hull, Quebec, Canadian Centre For Folk Culture Studies, Canadian Museum of Civilization.

TRANSCRIPTION SYMBOLS

The texts in this volume are recorded directly from my informants' oral rendition. In order to transfer the text to the page in an orderly and readable fashion, I have relied on the following symbols:

[...] and [....]	= editor's deletion;
... and	= informant's ellipsis;
..	= incomplete word;
—	= hesitation;
..—	= incomplete word followed by hesitation;
.. ... or	= incomplete word followed by informant's ellipsis;
/ /	= probable, but not clearly-heard, words.

Incomplete words shown in the English text are based on a translation of what I surmise the complete Icelandic word would be. When unable to determine the meaning of a partial word in the original text, I have transferred the Icelandic word fragment, intact, to the English text.

RHYMES ABOUT FAMILIAR ANIMALS AND PETS

1

Fuglinn í fjörunni,
hann heitir már.
Silkibleik er húfan hans
og gult undir hár.
Er sá fuglinn ekki smár,
bæði digur og fótahár.
Á bringunni svartur-- á bakinu svartur,
á bringunni grár.
Bröltir hann oft í snörunni,
fuglinn í fjörunni.

. . . . .

The bird on the beach
His name is Gull.
His cap is silky pale
And the hair under is yellow.
This bird is not small,
Both stout and long-legged.
His chest is black-- his back is black,
His chest is gray.
He often tumbles about in the snare;
The bird on the beach.

                    Mrs. Hrund Skúlason
                    Winnipeg, Manitoba

2*

Krummi krúnkar úti,
kallar á nafna sinn:
„Ég fann höfuđ af hrúti,
hrygg og gæruskinn."

. . . . .

Crook-beak croaks outside
Calls to his namesake:
"I found the head of a ram,
A spine and a fleece."

Mrs. Fríđa Holm
Vancouver, British Columbia

---

* See music transcription for this item on page 299.

3

Við skulum róa sjóinn á,
að sækja okkur ýsu.
En ef hann krummi kemur þá,
og kallar á hana Dísu?

. . . . .

Let's row out to sea
To fetch us a haddock.
But what if Crook-beak comes then
And calls for Dísa?

Mrs. Sigíður Björnsson
Gimli, Manitoba

4

Hún kisa og hann krummi,
hvar voru þau í nótt?
Kisa var inni í búri,
en krummi var úti á tóft.

. . . . .

Kitty and Crook-beak,
Where were they last night?
Kitty was in the pantry,
But Crook-beak was out on the ruins.

> Mrs. Sigiríður Björnsson
> Gimli, Manitoba

5

Litlu lömbin leika sér
létt um græna haga,
ef að grimmur ekki er
úlfur þeim til baga.

. . . . .

The little lambs play
Lightly about green pastures,
If only the angry
Wolf doesn't cause them harm.

                            Mr. Jón Mýrdal
                            Blaine, Washington

6

Fljúga hvítu fiðrildin
fyrir utan glugga,
hérna siglir einhver inn,
ofurlítil dugga.

. . . . .

The white butterflies fly
Outside the window.
Now there sails in here
A very small boat.

Mrs. Sigurveig Sveinsson
Baldur, Manitoba

Rhymes About Familiar Animals and Pets

7*

Það var amma mín. Hún hét Sigurbjörg, frá Sólheimum í Skagafirði, held ég hún hafi verið. Ég held það sé í Skagafirði. Hún hafði verið gefin fyrir hesta og mjög lagin á hestbaki, og orti vísu um reiðhestinn sinn:

    Aldrei mun ég eignast hest   [Gunnlaugur Holm recites.]
    annan eins með snilli,
    litli Rauður ber mig best
    bæjanna á milli.
    „Litla Jörp með lipran fót."   [G.H. to Fríða Holm.]
    Litla Jörp með lipran fót   [G.H. sings.]
    labbar götu þvera;
    hún mun seinna á mannamót
    mig í söðli bera.   [G.H. and F.H. sing.]

. . . . .

It was my grandmother, her name was Sigurbjörg, from Sólheimar in Skagafjörður, I think it was. I think it is in Skagafjörður. She liked horses and was very good on horseback, and she composed a verse about her horse:

    Never again will I own a horse   [Gunnlaugur Holm recites.]
    As excellent as this one.
    Little Rauður carries me best
    Between farmsteads.
    "Little Jörp with limber leg."   [G.H. to Fríða Holm.]
    Little Jörp with limber leg   [G.H. sings.]
    Walks across the road.
    Later to gatherings of men
    She will carry me, sidesaddle.   [G.H. and F.H. sing.]

                                  Mr. Gunnlaugur Holm
                                  Mrs. Fríða Holm
                                  Vancouver, British Columbia

---

* See music transcription for this item on page 299.

8*

Gráa hestinn met ég minn
meir en prest í stólnum,
þó að lestur semji sinn,
sé í besta kjólnum.

. . . . .

I value my grey horse
More than a priest in the pulpit,
Even when, composing his sermon,
He wears his best coat.

Mr. Páll Hallson
Winnipeg, Manitoba

---

* See music transcription for this item on page 300.

9

Rauður minn er sterkur, stór,
stinnur vel til ferðalags,
suður á landið feitur fór,
fallegur á tagl og fax.

. . . . .

My Rauður is strong and big,
Quite solid for travel;
He went south, well fattened,
Fair of tail and mane.

Mr. Jón Pálsson
Arborg, Manitoba

10*

Afi minn fór á honum Rauđ
eitthvađ suđur á bæi,
sækja bæđi sykur og brauđ,
sitt af hvoru tagi.

. . . . .

Grandfather went on Rauđur
Toward the south-lying farms,
To fetch both sugar and bread,
Some of each.

**Mrs. Fríđa Holm
Vancouver, British Columbia**

---

* See music transcription for this item on page 300.

11

Fallega Skjóni fótinn ber
framan eftir hlíðunum,
af góðum var hann gefinn mér;
gaman er að ríða honum.

. . . . .

Fairly Skjóni moves his leg
Forward along the slopes.
By good people he was given me;
What fun it is to ride him.

Mr. Jón Pálsson
Arborg, Manitoba

12

Litli Skjóni leikur sér,
lipurt hefur fótatak.
Pabbi góður gaf hann mér,
gaman er að koma á bak.

. . . . .

Little Skjóni plays about,
Nimble is his step.
My good papa gave him to me;
What fun it is to mount him.

**Mr. Jón Pálsson
Arborg, Manitoba**

RIGMAROLES

Rigmaroles 33

13

Árni, Hjalti, Auđunn, Steinn,
Oddur, Bjarni, Torfi, Jón,
Grímur, Högni, Gestur, Sveinn,
Gunnar, Skeggi, Björn, Símon.

Valdimar Johnson
Riverton, Manitoba

14

Sigga, Vigga, Sunneva,
Salka, Valka, Halldóra,
Þórunn, Jórunn, Þórkatla,
Þorbjörg, Vilborg, Arnóra.

Mr. Jón Pálsson
Arborg, Manitoba

15

Táta, táta,
teldu bræður þína.
Einn og tveir,
inn komu þeir.
Þrír og fjórir,
furðu stórir.
Fimm og sex,
sjö og átta,
síðan fóru þeir að hátta.
Og um miðjan mo.. . . . . .
Níu, tíu, ellefu, tólf,
síðan fóru þeir að sofa,
sína drauma að lofa.
Og um miðjan morgunn,
mamma vakti þá:
þrettán, fjórtán,
fimmtán, sextán,
fætur stukku þeir á.
Síðan fóru þeir að smala
suður fyrir á.
Sautján, átján,
lambærnar fundu þeir þá.
Nítján voru tvílembdar
torfunum á.
Tuttugu sauðirnir
suður við sel.
Teldu nú áfram
og teldu nú vel.

. . . . .

Little girl, little girl,
count your brothers.
One and two
came in.
Three and four,
Amazingly big.
Five and six,
Seven and eight,
Then they went to bed.
And at mid-mo.. . . . .
Nine, ten, eleven, twelve,
Then they went to sleep,
Their dreams to commend.
And at mid-morning,
Mamma woke them up.
Thirteen, fourteen,
Fifteen, sixteen,
They jumped to their feet.
Then they started herding
South of the river.
Seventeen, eighteen,
They then found the lamb-bearing ewes.
Nineteen bore two lambs each
On the turf.
Twenty wethers were
South by the summer dairy.
Now, keep counting
And count well.

Mrs. Steinunn Bjarnason
Arborg, Manitoba

16

Táta, táta,
teldu dætur þínar.
Hægt er að telja:
tvær eru í helju,
þrjár matseljur,
fjórar í búri
borð að reisa,
fimm í fjalli
fífil að grafa,
átta í eyjum
eld að kynda,
tíu í túni
og tuttugu eru heima,
níutíu hlaupa
eftir ömmunni sinni,
skrúnkunni gömlu.
Hálft er nú talið,
telja má ég lengur:
hundrað eru á húsabaki,
þrjár eru mínar Þórur,
og fjórar Þórgunnur,
átta Ólöfur,
þrjátíu Þuríður
og þrettán Gróur.

. . . . .

Girly, girly,
count your daughters.

It's easy to count:
Two are in the land of the dead,
Three are cooks,
Four in the pantry
Setting up a table,
Five on the mountain
Burying a dandelion,
Eight in the islands
Feeding a fire,
Ten in the home-field
And twenty are at home,
Ninety run
After their grandmother,
The old hag.
Half are now counted,
I can count further:
A hundred are behind the house,
Three are my Þóras
And four Þórgunnas,
Eight Ólöfs,
Thirty Þuríðurs
And thirteen Gróas.

Mr. Valdimar Johnson
Riverton, Manitoba

17

Draum dreymdi mig dag fyrir lítinn,
af þeim draumi drjúgt er að segja:
hvalur þótti mér á heiðum belja,
að þeim beljum sátu rekkar,
af þeim rekkum runnu dreyrar,
af þeim dreyrum drukku hrafnar,
af þeim hröfnum hriktir í vindi,
af þeim vindi veður í skýjum,
af þeim skýjum skein einn máni,
af þeim mána mjög ljós himinn,
á þeim himni heiðar stjörnur,
á þeim stjörnum stóðu laukar,
að þeim laukum léku meyjar
um löndin öll og eyjar.

Þá er það búið.

. . . . .

I dreamt a dream a short while ago,
Of that dream there are many things to report:
It seemed to me a whale bellowed up on the heaths,
Men sat watching over those cows,
Blood ran off those men,
Ravens drank off that blood,
In the winds those ravens creak,
From that wind turmoil in clouds,
A moon shone off those clouds,
A very bright sky from that moon,
Bright stars in that sky,
Leeks stood out on those stars,

> Maidens played with those leeks
> Over all the lands and islands.

Then that's finished.

Mrs. Dagbjört Vopnfjörd
Blaine, Washington

18

Þegiðu, þegiðu sonur minn sæli
þangað til að kýr okkar koma af fjalli.
Heim koma þær Hringa og Stjarna,
Dúfa og Dalla, drynja heim allar,
Íla og hún Ála, ofan frá skála,
Flekka og hún Fræna fylla þær skjólur;
Geit og hún Grana ganga í hellir.
(Hver býr í helli, hornum skellir?
    - Sí-spítandi hamramóðir.)
Lykla og Lína og Langspena,
Komnar eru Krúna og Kreppilhyrna,
og Mjóhyrna sem mjólkar best
í kútinn handa börnunum;
Gullinhyrna gengur fyrir þeim öllum;
Gönguhryggja gengur fram á dal.
Þar skokkar á eftir
Skinnbrók og Skorungur og Skolamaki,
Hnífill og Stiffur og Velbrokkandi.

. . . . .

Be quiet, be quiet my happy son
Until our cows come off the mountain.
Home come Hringa and Stjarna,
Dúfa and Dalla, all troop home,
Íla and Ála, from above the shieling,
Flekka and Fræna, they fill pails;
Geit and Grana walk into a cave.
(Who dwells in a cave, clips horns?
    - The ever-spitting cliff-mother.)

Lykla and Lína and Langspena,
Krúna and Kreppilhyrna have come,
And Mjóhyrna who gives the most milk
Into the cask for the children.
Gullinhyrna walks ahead of them all;
Gönguhryggja walks into the valley.
Hopping behind them are
Skinnbrók and Skorungur and Skolamaki,
Hnífill and Stiffur and Velbrokkandi.

Mrs. Sigurveig Sveinsson
Baldur, Manitoba

19

Heyrði ég í hamrinum
hátt var þar látið,
sárt var þar grátið.
Búkonan dillaði börnunum öllum:
Ingunni, Tjingunni,
Jórunni, Þórunni,
Básunni, Dísunni,
Völkunni, Sölkunni,
Eðalvarði, Ormagarði,
Eiríki og Sveini,
óx undir steini.
 Ekki heiti ég Eiríkur
þó ég sé það kallaður.
Ég er sonur Sylgju
sem bar mig undan bylgju.
Bylgjan og báran
brutu mínar árar
langt út á sjó,
langt út á miðjum sjó,
með hornin fögur og mjö."

. . . . .

I heard in the cliff,
Loud carryings-on,
Bitter crying.
The housewife lulled all the children:
Ingunn, Tjingunn,
Jórunn, Thórunn,

Bása, Dísa,
Valka, Salka,
Eðalvarður, Ormagarður,
Eiríkur and Sveinn,
Grew under a rock.
"My name is not Eiríkur
Although that's what I'm called.
I am the son of Sylgja
Who bore me from under a wave.
The wave and the billow
Broke my oars
Far out at sea,
Far out in the middle of the sea
With horns fair and slender.

Mrs. Steinunn Bjarnason
Arborg, Manitoba

20

Ekki heiti ég Eiríkur
þo ég sé það kallaður.
Ég er sonur Sylgju
sem bar mig undan bylgju.
Bylgjurnar báðar
brutu mínar árar
Langt út á sjó.
Hallast á hesti mínum,
ríða vil ég þó.
Allar mínar sorgir
batt ég undir skó.

. . . . .

My name is not Eiríkur
Although that is what I'm called.
I am the son of Sylgja
Who bore me from under a wave.
Both the waves
Broke my oars
Far out at sea.
My horse's load shifts,
But still I will ride.
All my sorrows
I tied under my shoe.

Mrs. Sigurveig Sveinsson
Baldur, Manitoba

21

/Komdu til mín/ fyrsta kvöld jóla;
ég skal gefa þér einn fisk
– allt upp á einn disk.
Komdu til mín annað kvöld jóla;
ég skal gefa þér tvö hænsni,
einn fisk
– allt upp á einn disk.
Komdu til mín þriðja kvöld jóla;
ég skal gefa þér þrjár kökur,
tvö hænsni,
einn fisk
– allt upp á einn disk.
Komdu til mín fjórða kvöld jóla;
ég skal gefa þér fjögur föll,
þrjár kökur,
tvö hænsni,
einn fisk
– allt upp á einn disk.
Komdu til mín fimmta kvöld jóla;
ég skal gefa þér fimm feit,
fjögur föll,
þrjar kökur,
tvö hænsni,
einn fisk
– allt upp á einn disk.
Komdu til mín kvöl. .-- sjötta kvöld jóla;
ég skal gefa þér svín með sex grísum,
fimm feit,
fjögur föll,
þrjár kökur,

tvö hænsni,
einn fisk
– allt upp á einn disk.
Komdu til mín sjöunda kvöld jóla;
ég skal gefa þér sjö saltsæði,
svín með sex grísum,
fimm feit,
fjögur föll,
þrjár kökur,
tvö hænsni,
einn fisk
– allt upp á einn disk.
Komdu til mín áttunda kvöld jóla;
ég skal gefa þér átta uxa með ökrum,
sjö saltsæði,
svín með sex grísum,
fimm feit,
fjögur föll,
þrjár kökur,
tvö hænsni,
einn fisk
– allt upp á einn disk.
Komdu til mín níunda kvöld jóla;
ég skal gefa þér níu geitur upphyrndar,
átta uxa með ökrum,
sjö saltsæði,
svín með sex grísum,
fimm feit,
fjögur föll,
þrjár kökur,

tvö hænsni,
einn fisk
– allt upp á einn disk.
Komdu til mín tíunda kvöld jóla;
ég skal gefa þér tíu kýrnar snemmbærar,
níu geitur upphyrndar,
átta uxa með ökrum,
sjö saltsæði,
svín með sex grísum,
fimm feit,
fjögur föll,
þrjár kökur,
tvö hænsni,
einn fisk
– allt upp á einn disk.
Komdu til mín ellefta kvöld jóla,
ég skal gefa þér ellefu kapla filfulla,
tíu kýrnar snemmbærar,
níu geitur upphyrndar,
átta uxa með ökrum,
sjö saltsæði,
svín með sex grísum,
fimm feit,
fjögur föll,
þrjár kökur,
tvö hænsni,
einn fisk
– allt upp á einn disk.

. . . . .

/Come to me/ the first eve of yule;

Rigmaroles

I will give you one fish
– All on one dish.
Come to me the second eve of yule;
I will give you two fowl,
One fish
– All on one dish.
Come to me the third eve of yule;
I will give you three cakes,
Two fowl,
One fish
– All on one dish.
Come to me the fourth eve of yule;
I will give you four slaughtered sheep,
Three cakes,
Two fowl,
One fish
– All on one dish
Come to me the fifth eve of yule;
I will give you five casks
Four slaughtered sheep,
Three cakes,
Two fowl,
One fish
– All on one dish.
Come to me ev. .-- sixth eve of yule;
I will give you a sow with six piggies
Five casks,
Four slaughtered sheep,
Three cakes,
Two fowl,
One fish
– All on one dish.

Come to me the seventh eve of yule;
I will give you seven salt-seeds,
A sow with six piggies,
Five cakes,
Four slaughtered sheep,
Three cakes,
Two fowl,
One fish
– All on one dish.
Come to me the eighth eve of yule;
I will give you eight oxen with grain fields,
Seven salt-seeds,
A sow with six piggies,
Five casks,
Four slaughtered sheep,
Three cakes,
Two fowl,
One fish
– All on one dish.
Come to me the ninth eve of yule;
I will give you nine straight-horned goats,
Eight oxen with grain fields,
Seven salt-seeds,
A sow with six piggies,
Five casks,
Four slaughtered sheep,
Three cakes,
Two fowl,
One fish
– All on one dish.
Come to me the tenth eve of yule;
I will give you ten early-bearing cows,

Nine straight-horned goats,
Eight oxen with grain fields,
Seven salt-seeds,
A sow with six piggies,
Five casks,
Four slaughtered sheep,
Three cakes,
Two fowl,
One fish
– All on one dish.
Come to me the eleventh eve of yule;
I will give you eleven mares in foal,
Ten early-calving cows,
Nine straight-horned goats,
Eight oxen with grain fields,
Seven salt-seeds,
A sow with six piggies,
Five casks,
Four slaughtered sheep,
Three cakes,
Two fowl,
One fish
– All on one dish.

Mrs. Sigríður Björnsson
Gimli, Manitoba

22

Karl var að berja fisk út við stein og þá kom lítill fugl og vildi fá sér mola í nefið, svo karl hjó af honum nefið. Hann bað hann að gefa sér þráðarspotta að hnýta um nefið, og karl vísaði honum til kerlingar.

"Ekki geri ég það," segir kerling.

"Þá skal melur koma og éta vef þinn. Melur komdu og éttu vef kerlingar, kerling vill ekki gefa mér rauðan þráðarspotta að hnýta um nefið, því karl hjó af mér nefið."

"Ekki geri ég það," segir melur.

"Þá skal mús koma og éta þig. Mús komdu og éttu mel, melur vill ekki éta vef kerlingar, kerling vill ekki gefa mér rauðan þráðarspotta að hnýta um nefið, en karl hjó af mér nefið."

"Ekki geri ég það," segir mús.

"Þá skal köttur koma og éta þig. Köttur komdu og éttu mús, mús vill ekki éta mel, melur vill ekki éta vef kerlingar, kerling vill ekki gefa mér rauðan þráðarspotta að hnýta um nefið, en karl hjó af mér nefið."

"Ekki geri ég það," segir köttur.

"Þá skal hundur koma og rífa þig. Hundur komdu og rífðu kött, köttur vill ekki éta mús, mús vill ekki éta mel, melur vill ekki éta vef kerlingar, kerling vill ekki gefa mér rauðan þráðarspotta að hnýta um nefið, en karl hjó af mér nefið."

"Ekki geri ég það," segir hundur.

"Þá skal vöndur koma og hýða þig. Vöndur komdu og hýddu hund, hundur vill ekki rífa kött, köttur vill ekki éta mús, mús vill ekki éta mel, melur vill ekki éta vef kerlingar, kerling vill ekki gefa mér rauðan þráðarspotta að hnýta um nefið, en karl hjó af mér nefið."

"Ekki geri ég það," segir vöndur.

"Þá skal eldur koma og brenna þig. Eldur komdu og brenndu vönd, vöndur vill ekki hýða hund, hundur vill ekki rífa kött, köttur vill ekki éta mús, mús vill ekki éta mel, melur vill ekki éta vef kerlingar, kerling vill ekki gefa mér rauðan þráðarspotta að hnýta um nefið, en karl hjó af mér nefið."

"Ekki geri ég það," segir eldur

„Þá skal vatn koma og slökkva þig. Vatn komdu og slökktu eld, eldur vill ekki brenna vönd, vöndur vill ekki hýða hund, hundur vill ekki rífa kött, köttur vill ekki éta mús, mús vill ekki éta mel, melur vill ekki éta vef kerlingar, kerling vill ekki gefa mér rauðan þráðarspotta að hnýta um nefið, en karl hjó af mér nefið."

„Ekki geri ég það," segir vatn.

„Þá skal boli koma og drekka þig. Boli komdu og drekktu vatn, vatn vill ekki slökkva eld, eldur vill ekki brenna vönd, vöndur vill ekki hýða hund, hundur vill ekki rífa kött, köttur vill ekki éta mús, mús vill ekki éta mel, melur vill ekki éta vef kerlingar, kerling vill ekki gefa mér rauðan þráðarspotta að hnýta um nefið, en karl hjó af mér nefið."

„Ekki geri ég það," segir boli.

„Þá skal klafi koma að hengja þig. Klafi komdu og hengdu bola, boli vill ekki drekka vatn, vatn vill ekki slökkva eld, eldur vill ekki brenna vönd, vöndur vill ekki hýða hund, hundur vill ekki rífa kött, köttur vill ekki éta mús, mús vill ekki éta mel, melur vill ekki éta vef kerlingar, kerling vill ekki gefa mér rauðan þráðarspotta að binda um nefið, karl hjó af mér nefið."

„Ekki geri ég það," segir klafi.

„Þá skal öxi koma og höggva þig. Öxi komdu og höggðu klafa, klafi vill ekki hengja bola, boli vill ekki drekka vatn, vatn vill ekki slökkva eld, eldur vill ekki hýða hund, hundur vill ekki rífa kött, köttur vill ekki éta mús, mús vill ekki éta mel, melur vill ekki éta vef kerlingar, kerling vill ekki gefa mér raudan þráðarspotta að hnýta um nefið, en karl hjó af mér nefið."

„Ekki geri ég það," segir öxi.

„Þá skal brýni koma og brýna þig. Brýni komdu og brýndu öxi, öxi vill ekki höggva klafa, klafi vill ekki hengja bola, boli vill ekki drekka vatn, vatn vill ekki slökkva eld, eldur vill ekki brenna vönd, vöndur vill ekki hýða hund, hundur vill ekki rífa kött, köttur vill ekki éta mús, mús vill ekki éta mel kerlingar-- vef kerlingar. Mús vill ekki éta mel, melur vill ekki éta vef kerlingar, kerling vill ekki gefa mér rauðan þráðarspotta að hnýta um nefið, en karl hjó af mér nefið."

• „Það skal ég gera," segir brýnið.

„Brýnið brýndi öxi, öxi hjó klafa, klafi hengdi bola, boli drakk vatn, vatn slökkti eld, eldur brenndi vönd, vöndur hýddi hund, hundur reif kött, köttur át mús, mús át mel, melur át vef kerlingar, kerling gaf mér rauðan þráðarspotta að hnýta um nefið, og þá greri nefið."

. . . . .

Churl was pounding a fish out by a stone, and a little bird came and wanted a crumb in his beak, so Churl chopped off his beak. He asked him to give him a piece of red thread to tie about his beak, but Churl sent him to Crone.

"I won't do that," says Crone.

"Then Moth will come and eat your weave. Moth come and eat Crone's weave, Crone won't give me a piece of red thread to tie about my beak, because Churl chopped off my nose."

"I won't do that," says Moth.

"Then Mouse will come and eat you. Mouse come and eat Moth, Moth won't eat Crone's weave, Crone won't give me a piece of red thread to tie about the beak, but Churl chopped off my nose."

"I won't do that," says Mouse.

"Then Cat will come and eat you. Cat come and eat Mouse, Mouse won't eat Moth, Moth won't eat Crone's weave, Crone won't give me a piece of red thread to tie about the beak, but Churl chopped off my beak."

"I won't do that," says Cat.

"Then Dog will come and bite you. Dog come and bite Cat, Cat won't eat Mouse, Mouse won't eat Moth, Moth won't eat Crone's weave, Crone won't give me a piece of red thread to tie about the beak, but Churl chopped off my beak."

"I won't do that," says Dog.

"Then Whip will come and whip you. Whip come and whip Dog, Dog won't bite Cat, Cat won't eat Mouse, Mouse won't eat Moth, Moth won't eat Crone's weave, Crone won't give me a piece of red thread to tie about the beak, but Churl chopped off my beak."

"I won't do that," says Whip.

"Then Fire will come and burn you. Fire come and burn Whip, Whip won't whip Dog, Dog won't bite Cat, Cat won't eat Mouse, Mouse won't eat Moth, Moth won't eat Crone's weave, Crone won't give me a piece of red thread to tie about the beak, but Churl chopped off my beak."

"I won't do that," says Fire.

"Then Water will come and put you out. Water come and put Fire out, Fire won't burn Whip, Whip won't whip Dog, Dog won't bite Cat, Cat won't eat Mouse, Mouse won't eat Moth, Moth won't eat Crone's weave, Crone won't give me a piece of red thread to tie about the beak, but Churl chopped off my beak."

"I won't do that," says Water.

"Then Bull will come and drink you. Bull come and drink Water, Water won't put Fire out, Fire won't burn Whip, Whip won't whip Dog, Dog won't bite

Cat, Cat won't eat Mouse, Mouse won't eat Moth, Moth won't eat Crone's weave, Crone won't give me a piece of red thread to tie about the beak, but Churl chopped off my beak."

"I won't do that," says Bull.

"Then Yoke will come and choke you. Yoke come and choke Bull, Bull won't drink Water, Water won't put Fire out, Fire won't burn Whip, Whip won't whip Dog, Dog won't bite Cat, Cat won't eat Mouse, Mouse won't eat Moth, Moth won't eat Crone's weave, Crone won't give me a piece of red thread to tie about the beak, Churl chopped off my beak."

"I won't do that," says Yoke.

"Then Ax will come and chop you. Ax come and chop Yoke, Yoke won't choke Bull, Bull won't drink Water, Water won't put Fire out, Fire won't whip Dog, Dog won't bite Cat, Cat won't eat Mouse, Mouse won't eat Moth, Moth won't eat Crone's weave, Crone won't give me a piece of red thread to tie about the beak, but Churl chopped off my beak."

"I won't do that," says Ax.

"Then Whetstone will come and sharpen you. Whetstone come and sharpen Ax, Ax won't chop Yoke, Yoke won't choke Bull, Bull won't drink Water, Water won't put out Fire, Fire won't burn Whip, Whip won't whip Dog,

Dog won't bite Cat, Cat won't eat Mouse, Mouse won't eat Crone's Moth--Crone's weave. Mouse won't eat Moth, Moth won't eat Crone's weave, Crone won't give me a piece of red thread to tie about the nose, but Churl chopped off my beak."

"That I will do," says Whetstone. Whetstone sharpened Ax, Ax chopped Yoke, Yoke choked Bull, Bull drank Water, Water put Fire out, Fire burned Whip, Whip whipped Dog, Dog bit Cat, Cat ate Mouse, Mouse ate Moth, Moth ate Crone's weave, Crone gave me a piece of red thread to tie about the beak, and then the beak healed.

Mrs. Sigríður Björnsson
Gimli, Manitoba

23

M.E.: Það eru hjón sem eignast þrjár dætur.

Sigmundur Helgason: Já. Og-- og fyrsta dóttirin heitir Sip, og önnur dóttirin hét Sipsippinip, og þriðja dóttirin hét Sipsippinipsipsúrumsip.

En svo voru það önnur hjón sem eignuðust þrjá drengi, og fyrsti strákurinn hét Skrat, og annar strákurinn hét Skratskratarat, og þriðji strákurinn hét Skratskrataratskratskrámuskrat.

Svo giftist þetta allt saman og Skrat átti Sip, og Skratskratarat átti Sipsippinip, og Skratskrataratskratskrámuskrat átti Sipsippinipsipsúrumsip. [Laughter.]

. . . . .

M.E.: There is a couple that beget three daughters.

S.H.: Yes. And-- and the name of the first daughter is Sip, and the second daughter was called Sipsippinip, and the third daughter was called Sipsippinip-sipsúrumsip.

But then there was another couple that begat three boys, and the first lad was called Skrat, and the second lad was called Skratskratarat, and the third lad was called Skratskrataratskratskrámuskrat

Then all of them got married and Skrat got Sip, and Skratskratarat got Sipsippinip, and Skratskrataratskratskrámuskrat got Sipsippinipsipsúrumsip.
 [Laughter.]

Mr. Sigmundur Helgason
Mozart, Saskatchewan

24

Og ke. .-- og-- og kýrin ætlaði að fara að eiga kálf.

Og kálfinn bar rangt að, svo að skottið kom fyrst (eða halinn, réttara sagt).

Og svo tók karlinn í halann og togaði, og ekkert gékk.

Og þá kom kerlingin og tók í karlinn,

og karlinn í kerlinguna,

og kerlingin í rófuna,

og ekkert gékk.

Og svo komu krakkarnir.

Og það var Einbein, tók í kerlinguna,

og kerlingin í karlinn,

karlinn í rófuna,

og ekkert gékk.

Og svo kom Tvíbein,

og Tvíbein í-- í Einbein,

og Einbein í-- í karl. .-- í kerlinguna,

og kerlingin í karlinn,

í rófuna,

og ekkert gékk.

Og þetta gékk svona. Ég man ekki hvað það voru orðnir margir, hvort það voru einir tólf. Og þetta varð voðalega mikill stafl, og-- og lang. .-- löng runa af . . . .

(Þó það skildi ekkert um-- þetta var ekkert til að skilja, þá bara þótti þeim [informant's children] gaman að heyra-- heyra það.

M.E.: Og haltu þá áfram.

Herdís Eiriksson: Ég er búin!

Tvíbein tók í Þríbein,
og Þríbein í Tvíbein,
og Tvíbein í Einbein,
og Einbein í-- í kerlinguna,
og kerlingin í karlinn.
Og ekkert gékk þangað til það var orðið Tólfbein.
Tólfbein togaði í Ellefubein
Ellefubein togaði í Tíubein,
Tíubein í Níubein,
Níubein í Áttabein,
Áttabein í Sjöbein,
Sjöbein í Sexbein,
Sexbein í Fimmbein,
Fimmbein í Fjórbein,
Fjórbein í Þríbein,
Þríbein í Tvíbein,
Tvíbein í Einbein. [Laughter.]
Einbein í kerlinguna,
kerlingin í karlinn,
og karlinn í rófuna,
og þá slitnaði rófan! [Laughter.]

Er þetta ekki vitlaust?

. . . . .

And cr. .-- and -- and the cow was going to calve.
And the calf came facing the wrong way, so the scut
    came first (or the tail, to be correct).
And then the churl grabbed the tail and pulled, and nothing
    worked.
And then the crone came and grabbed the churl,
And the churl tugged at the crone,
And the crone at the tail,

And nothing worked.
And then the kids came:
And that was Onebone, tugged at the crone,
And the crone at the churl,
And the churl at the tail,
And nothing worked.
And then came Twobone,
And Twobone at-- at Onebone,
And Onebone at-- at the chur. .-- at the crone,
And the crone at the churl,
At the tail,
And nothing worked.

And it went on like this. I don't remember how many there got to be, whether there were about twelve. And this was a huge stack, and-- and long. .-- long run of . . . .

(Although they [informant's children] didn't understand anything about-- there wasn't anything to understand, they just had fun hearing-- hearing it.

M.E.: So, continue then.

H.E.: I'm finished!
Twobone grabbed Threebone,
And Threebone at Twobone,
And Twobone at Onebone,
And Onebone at-- at the crone,
And the crone at the churl.
And nothing worked until it was Twelvebone.
Twelvebone pulled Elevenbone,
Elevenbone at Tenbone
Tenbone at Ninebone
Ninebone at Eightbone
Eightbone at Sevenbone
Sevenbone at Sixbone
Sixbone at Fivebone,

Fivebone at Fourbone,
Fourbone at Threebone,
Threebone at Twobone,
Twobone at Onebone. [Laughter.]
Onebone at the crone,
The crone at the churl,
And the churl at the tail,
And the tail came off! [Laughter.]

Isn't that crazy!

Mrs. Herdís Eiríksson
Arborg, Manitoba

25

Karl og kerling
riðu á alþing.
Þau fundu titling
og stungu í vettling.
Þegar þau komu heim
þeim var gefið bein,
brotið yfir stein.
Karl tók til orða
að mál væri að borða.
Þá kom inn fiskur-- diskur,
var á blautur fiskur,
silungur sætur
og fjórir sviðafætur.
Upp tók hann einn;
ekki var hann seinn,
gerist-- gerði úr honum mann
og Grettir heitir hann.
Margt kunni Grettir vel að vinna;
hann fór út til eyja
og svæfði þar meyjar,
kúr og kálfa
og keisarann sjálfann. [Laughter.]

. . . . .

A churl and a crone
Rode to parliament.
They found a sparrow
Stuck it in a mitten.
When they came home
They were given a bone

Broken on a stone.
The churl said
That it was time to eat.
Then in came a fish-- dish,
On it, a wet fish,
Sweet-tasting trout
And four sheep's feet.
He picked one up;
He wasn't slow
Makes-- made of it a man
And Grettir is his name.
Grettir could do many things well;
He went out to the islands
And put to sleep maidens,
Cows and calfs,
And Cæsar himself. [Laughter.]

Mr. Jón Howardson
Vancouver, British Columbia

26

Róum við á selinn
röstungs út á melinn.
Skjótum við og skjótum,
skreipt er undir fótum.
Við látum brokka,
vel gengur okkur.
Förum svo að halda í land
og kærum okkur ekki grand.
Þar situr Jói
hátt upp í stafni,
ofurlítill gói;
ég nefni hann með nafni.
Rösklega rær hann,
rekkum stærri nær hann,
fiski aflað fær hann,
fljóðum yndi ljær hann,
byssu fagra ber hann.
Birtings heiði fer hann,
selinn þegar sér hann,
síst ólipur er hann.
Um leið hæfir á hann,
af því hann vill fá hann.
Margur lofa má hann
minjaviðinn smáan.
Heldur leið að landi,
lítinn bát setjandi.
Fer ég að fjörusandi
með faðminn útbreiðandi.
Vinur minn af fleyi
velkominn ég segi.

Tíđum þađ ég þreyi
þig ađ líta megi.

Þetta er búiđ.

. . . . .

Let's row out a-sealing
On the plain of the walrus.*
We shoot and shoot,
It is slippery under foot.
We let it move on;
It goes well for us.
Then we start heading for land
And let nothing trouble us.
There Jói sits
High up in the prow,
The little lad;
I call him by name.
He rows briskly
Keeps up with the bigger lads,
He can catch fish,
He delights the lasses,
He carries a handsome gun.
He travels over the heath of the sea-trout.*
When he spots the seal
He is quite agile.
He immediately aims at him,
Because he wants to get him.

---

* Poetic circumlocution (kenning): the sea.
* Poetic circumlocution: the sea.

Rigmaroles

> Many will want to praise him,
> The small offspring.
> It heads for land;
> Beached is the small boat.
> I go to the sandy beach
> With arms spread out.
> My friend off the boat,
> I declare welcome.
> Frequently I long to
> Be allowed to see you.

It is finished.

Mrs. Þórey Björnsson
Mountain, North Dakota

27

Sat ég undir fiskihlaða föður míns;
átti ég að gæta bús og barna,
svíns og sauða.
Menn komu að mér,
ráku staf í hnakka minn,
gerðu mér svo mikinn skaða,
settu eld í bónda hlaða.
Hlaðinn tók að brenna,
ég tók að renna,
allt út undir lönd,
allt út undir biskups lönd.
Biskup átti valið bú,
hann gaf mér bæði uxa og kú.
Uxinn tók að vaxa
og kýrin að mjólka.
Sankti María gaf mér brauð,
síðan lá hún steindauð.
Önnur gaf mér Freyja
en sú kunni ekki að deyja.
Gott þótti mér út að líta
í skinninu hvíta og skikkjunni grænni.
Kona mín í kofanum,
hún bauð mér inn til stofu.
Ei vil ég til stofu gá,
heldur upp til Hóla
að hitta konu bónda.
Kona bónda gékk til brunns;
hún vagaði, kjagaði.
Lét hún ganga hettuna, smettuna,

Rigmaroles

Digga litla í Dimmadal.
Nú er dauður Egill og Kegill í Skógi.

. . . . .

I sat by my father's stack of fish;
I was to look after the farm and the children,
The swine and the sheep.
Men came at me,
Put a club to the back of my head,
Did me so much harm,
Set fire to the farmer's stack.
The stack began to burn,
I started running,
All the way out to the lands,
All the way out to the Bishop's lands.
The Bishop had a choice farm,
He gave me both an ox and a cow.
The ox started growing
And the cow to give milk.
Holy María gave me a sheep,
Then she fell down stone-dead.
Freyja gave me another one,
But that one didn't know how to die.
It was good to look out,
In the white fur and the green cape.
My wife in the cottage,
She invited me into the sitting-room.
I don't want to look into the sitting-room,
But rather up to Hólar

To meet the farmer's wife.
The farmer's wife walked to the well;
She waddled, she paddled.
She let hood and face agitate,
Little Digga of Dimmadal.
Now Egill and Kegill of Skógur are dead.

Mr. Jón Howardson
Vancouver, British Columbia

28

Í fyrravetur fyrir jólin
fann ég hann Pál minn Bjarnason.
Þá skein mitt í suðri sólin,
setti ég á hann mína von.
Kátur var hann kjöt að brytja;
kátur bauð hann mér að sitja.
Lítillátur lækkaði hann sig,
lagði sessinn undir mig.
Upp tók baukinn eyðir spanga
og í nefið tók á sér,
en þá tók ég að mögla og manga
því maðurinn gaf ei parið mér.
En síðan var mér sent á diski
selkorn nokkuð og lungnablað,
þind af sauði og framan af fiski;
fært var mér það út á hlað.
Út í fjós fýsti mig að róla,
stóð þar full af soði fyrir mér skjóla.
Brenndi ég allann munninn minn
því engan fann ég eysilinn,
og þá fór ég að góla.

. . . . .

Last winter before Christmas
I came upon my dear friend Páll Bjarnason.
The sun then shone directly in the south;
I set my heart on him.
Merrily he was cutting meat,
Merrily he invited me to sit.
Modestly he lowered himself;

Placed the cushion under me.
The man took out his snuff box,
And put some in his nose,
But then I started to complain and haggle
Because the man wouldn't give me any.
But later there was sent to me, on a platter,
The midriff of a sheep and the head of a fish;
It was brought to me in the courtyard.
I wanted to wander out to the byre,
A full pail of broth stood there before me.
I burned my whole mouth
Because I couldn't find a ladle,
And then I started howling.

                              Mrs. Guðrún Pálsson
                              Arborg, Manitoba

29

Tunglið, tunglið taktu mig
berðu mig upp til skýja,
því þar situr hún móðir mín
og kembir ull nýja.
Þar sitja nunnur
og skafa gulltunnur,
og þar sitja Jónar
og skafa gullprjóna,
og þar situr hann afi minn
og skefur gamla hattinn sinn.

Aumingja karlinn!

. . . . .

Moon, moon take me up,
Carry me up to the clouds
Because there sits my mother
And cards raw wool.
There sit nuns and scrape gold casks,
And there sit Jónar
And scrape gold knitting needles,
And there sits my grandfather
And wipes his old hat.

Poor old fellow!

Mrs. Hrund Skúlason
Winnipeg, Manitoba

30

Stúlkurnar ganga sunnan með sjó
með línsvuntur langar og léreftin mjó.
Það mun vera stúlkan mín sem á undan gengur;
hún ber gull og festispennu ofan á belti.
Laufaprjóna ber hún þrjá.
Fögur er hún framan á,
með gullspöng um ennið;
það sómir henni,
stúlkunni minni.
Hún er skír og skemmtileg;
hún er dýr og dásamleg.
Hún gengur hógvær hvert sinn um bæinn,
litfríð og ráðsvinn.Reyna mun það hug minn
hvenær sem ég hljóð finn;
Þagnar allur þankinn.
Þá er úti hryggðin
og hver mannastyggð.

. . . . .

The girls walk south along the sea
With long cotton aprons and narrow linen scarfs.
That will be my girl who walks in front;
She carries jewelry and a necklace down to her belt.
She wears three leaf-shaped pins.
She is fair to look at,
With a gold spangle about her forehead;
It becomes her,
My girl.
She is bright and entertaining;
She is precious and adorable.

She always walks modestly about the house,
Fair-complexioned and virtuous.
It will try my mind
Whenever I hear a noise;
All thinking stops.
Then all sorrow vanishes
And every human resentment.

                                  Mrs. Jóhanna Sölvason
                                  Mozart, Saskatchewan

NONSENSE RHYMES

31

Séð hef ég páska setta um jól,
sveinbarn fætt í elli,
myrk. .-- myrkur björt, en svört var sól,
sund á hörðum velli.

. . . . .

I have seen Easter celebrated at yule,
A male child born in old age,
Dark. .-- darkness bright, and the sun was black,
Swimming done on a hard plain.

Mr. Valdimar Johnson
Riverton, Manitoba

32

Aldrei sofið er um nótt
en um daga svarta,
þá er allt svo hægt og hljótt
hvergi um neitt að kvarta.

. . . . .

One never sleeps at night,
But rather during the dark of day,
Then everything is so calm and quiet;
Nowhere anything to complain about.

Waldimar Johnson
Wynyard, Saskatchewan

33

Séð hef ég úr söltum sjó
suma reipin flétta.
Gott er að hafa gler í skó
þá gengið er í kletta.

. . . . .

I have seen from the salt sea
Some people braid rope.
It is good to have glass in one's shoes
When walking on rocks.

Mr. Lárus Nordal
Gimli, Manitoba

34

Blindir dæma best um lit.
Bárur í vindi þegja.
Í kálfunum er kóngavit.
Kýrnar frá mörgu segja.

. . . . .

The blind judge colour best.
Waves are silent in the wind.
Calfs have the wisdom of kings.
Cows have many things to report.

Mr. Valdimar Johnson
Riverton, Manitoba

Nonsense Rhymes

35

Í eld er best að ausa snjó,
eykst hans lag við þetta.
Gott er að hafa gler í skó,
þá gang. .-- gengið er í kletta.

. . . . .

It is best to shovel snow on fire,
Its form becomes larger, thereby.
It is good to put glass in one's shoes
When walk. .-- walking on rocks.

**Mrs. Jóhanna Thorkelsson
Arnes, Manitoba**

36

Hafa þeir dún í hafskipin,
hreina gler í möstrin stinn.
Elta þeir dúninn eins og skinn,
í ólar rista fuglsbeinin.

. . . . .

Ocean vessels are made of down,
The strong masts of clear glass.
Down is curried like a hide,
Bones of birds slit into thongs.

**Mrs. Sigríður Björnsson
Gimli, Manitoba**

37

Eitur er gott í augnarann
ýrt með dropa feitann.
Það er gott fyrir þyrstan mann
að þamba kopar heitann.

. . . . .

Poison is good for the eye,
Sprinkled with a fat glob.
It is good for a thirsty man
To quaff hot kopper.

Mrs. Sigurvieg Sveinsson
Baldur, Manitoba

38

Blý er gott í beitta þjöl.
Boginn stein má rétta.
Í fjöllunum vaxa frekar söl.
Í fjörunni grösin spretta.

` ` ` ` `

Lead is good in a sharp-edged file.
A bent stone can be straightened.
Dulse is more likely to grow in the mountains.
Herbal grasses grow on the beach.

Mrs. Sigurveig Sveinsson
Baldur, Manitoba

39

Séð hef ég flóna flóa mjólk.
Fallega lúsin hey upp bar.
Kýrnar bræða kerta tólg.
Ketið sjóða rjúpurnar.

. . . . .

I have seen the flea heat milk.
Beautifully the louse carried hay.
The cows melt candle tallow.
The ptarmigans boil meat.

                         Mrs. Sigurveig Sveinsson
                         Baldur, Manitoba

40

Séð hef ég köttinn syngja á bók,
selinn spinna hör á rokk,
skötuna elta skinn í brók,
úr skúmi prjóna smábandssokk.

. . . . .

I have seen the cat sing from a book,
The seal spin flax on a spinning wheel,
The skate curry a hide for a pair of breeches,
Knit a sock of fine yarn from twilight.

Mrs. Sigríður Björnsson
Gimli, Manitoba

41

Kisa spinnur bandið best.
Baulur kunna að saga.
Hrafninn oft á sjónum sést,
synda og fiskinn draga.

. . . . .

Kitty spins the best yarn.
Cows know how to saw.
The raven is often seen at sea,
Swimming and catching fish.

Mr. Valdimar Johnson
Riverton, Manitoba

42

Kött og tófu ég kyssast sá,
keldusvínið brýna ljá,
engil klifra upp úr gjá,
ær með byssum skjótast á.

` ` ` ` `

I saw a cat and a fox kiss,
The water-rail whet a scythe,
An angel climb out of a chasm,
Ewes with guns exchanging shots.

Mr. Valdimar Johnson
Riverton, Manitoba

43

Séð hef ég kapalinn eiga egg
og álftina folaldssjúka,
úr reyknum hlaðinn vænan vegg,
úr vatninu yst var kjúka.

. . . . .

I have seen the mare hatch an egg
And the swan heavy with foal,
A fine wall built with smoke,
Fresh cheese curdled from water.

                                              Mr. Lárus Nordal
                                              Gimli, Manitoba

44

Séð hef ég glíma sel og hest,
silunginn spinna allra best,
hrafninn synda á höfin út,
hákarlinn drekka úr brennivínskút.

. . . . .

I have seen a seal and a horse wrestle,
The trout spin best of all,
The raven swim out on the oceans,
The shark drinking from a brandy keg.

Mr. Valdimar Johnson
Riverton, Manitoba

45

Allra best er ull af sel,
æðardúnn í þvöru.
Maðkar syngja mikið vel.
Mýsnar éta tjöru.

. . . . .

The wool from a seal is best,
Eiderdown for a ladle.
Worms sing mighty well.
The mice eat tar.

Valdimar Johnson
Riverton, Manitoba

46

Fiskurinn hefur fögur hljóđ;
finnst hann oft á heiđum,
en ærnar renna eina slóđ
eftir snjónum breiđum.

. . . . .

The fish makes fair sounds;
He is often found on heaths,
But the ewes run along a single trail
Across the broad snowflats.

Mr. Lárus Nordal
Gimli, Manitoba

47

    Hákarlinn eftir hafinu rann,
    hár og digur júturinn.
    Inn í kórinn arkiði hann,
    klæddur rekabúturinn.

Sjáðu, þetta var ei. .-- eitt sem var satt.
Andrés Guðbjartsson: Nei. Það var ekkert satt í þessu.
Elísabet Guðbjartsson: Jú.
A.G.: Þetta er allt tóm lygi.
E.G.: Jú. "Hákarlinn eftir hafinu rann."
A.G.: Já. Það getur verið.
E.G.: [Laughter.]

. . . . .

    The shark ran over the ocean,
    The boil is tall and stout.
    Into the chancel he strode,
    The dressed-up piece of driftwood.

See, this was o. .-- one thing that was true.
A.G.: No. There was nothing true in this.
E.G.: Oh yes.
A.G.: This is all a big lie.
E.G.: Oh yes. "The shark ran over the ocean."
A.G.: Yes. It could be.
E.G.: [Laughter.]

                              Andrés Guðbjartsson
                              Elísabet Guðbjartsson
                              Hnausa, Manitoba

48

Elísabet Guðbjartsson: Svo er hin:
Séð hef ég . . .

Andrés Guðbjartsson: . . . kötturin . . . .

E.G.: Séð hef ég köttinn syngja á bók,
selinn spinna hör á rokk,
skötuna elta skinn í brók
og skúminn prjóna smábandssokk.

Þetta var allt sem ég kunni úr því.

M.E.: Þetta eru lygirímur; kallið þið það?
E.G. and A.G.: Lygirímur.
M.E.: Já. Hvað voru þær margar, þessar vísur?
A.G.: Þær voru margar.
M.E.: Hvað hét þessi maður?
A.G.: Ja. Það veit ég ekki.
M.E.: Þú sagðir-- hann-- átti að taka hann af?
A.G.: Já. Drepa.
M.E.: Og . . . ?
E.G.: Hann gerði eitthvað ljótt, sem að þeir ætluðu að . . . .
M.E.: Og hvað?
E.G.: Og þeir sögðu honum, ef hann yrkti svona margar vísur og það mundi-- og það mundi-- það ætti allt að vera lygji, nema þrjú orð sönn, og það var eitt-- eitt orðið, þetta: „Hákarlinn eftir hafinu rann." Svona. Hitt er allt lygi.
M.E.: Og slepptu þeir honum?
E.G.: Já.

. . . . .

Nonsense Rhymes

    E.G.: Then there is the other one:

                  I have seen . . .

    A.G.: . . . the cat . . . .

    E.G.   I have seen the cat sing from a book,
                        The seal spin flax on a spinning wheel,
                        The skate curry a hide for a pair of breeches,
                        And the skua knit a sock of yarn.

That is all I know of that.

    M.E.: These are lying rhymes, is that what you call them?
    E.G. and A.G.: Lying rhymes.
    M.E.: Yes. How many were there of these verses?
    A.G.: There were many.
    M.E.: What was the name of this man?
    A.G.: Ya. That I don't know.
    M.E.: You said-- he-- he was supposed to be executed?
    A.G.: Yes. Kill him.
    M.E.: And . . . ?
    E.G.: He did something ugly which they were going to . . . .
    M.E.: And what?
    E.G.: And they told him if he composed so many verses, and it would-- and it would-- it should all be a lie, except three truthful words, and that was one-- one word, this: "The shark ran over the ocean." Like that. All the rest is a lie.
    M.E.: And did they let him go?
    E.G.: Yes.

                                        Mrs. Elísabet Guðbjartsson
                                        Mr. Andrés Guðbjartsson
                                        Riverton, Manitoba

RIDDLES

49

Að kom ég þar elfan hörð
á var ferðum skjótum.
Undir vatni og ofan á jörð
arka ég þurrum fótum.

Þessi maður gékk undir foss.

. . . . .

I came to where the mighty river
Was on its speedy way.
Under water and over the ground
I walk with dry feet.

This man walked behind a waterfall.

Mr. Valdimar Johnson
Riverton, Manitoba

50

    Áđan sá ég úti þann
    sem á var bratt. .-- fattur kviđur,
    međ nefi sínu kroppa kann
    og kyngir engu nidur.

Þetta er heykrókur sem var brúkađur á Íslandi, hérna, fyrir hundrađ árum síđan.

. . . . .

    Just now I saw a fellow
    With a stee. .-- protruding belly.
    With his nose he can peck
    And he swallows nothing.

This was a hay hook that was used in Iceland, see here, a hundred years ago.

Mr. Valdimar Johnson
Riverton, Manitoba

51

Átta á fönnum ýtti,
allmargur það nýtti,
helzt þegar foldin fraus.
Á tuttugu hausum trýtti,
tíðum mjög sér flýtti;
öll voru augnalaus.
Eitt að auki var,
engin sá þess far.
Gettu gátu mín,
glögg er viskan þín.

Skaflajárnaður hestur.

. . . . .

Eight pushed ahead on the snow flats,
Many made use of it,
Especially when the ground froze.
Trod on twenty heads,
Often in a hurry,
All were without eyes.
There was one extra,
No one saw its trail.
Solve my riddle,
Sharp is your intelligence.

A rough-shod horse.

Mrs. Sigurveig Sveinsson
Baldur, Manitoba

52

    Ein er snót á yggjar mær
    ad mér kom í huga,
    hvad hún væri frökk og fær
    og fljót að yfirbuga.

Þetta er byssa.

    . . . . .

    There is a lady in the land of fear
    Who came to my mind;
    How bold and able she was
    And swift in overcoming.

This is a gun.

Mr. Valdimar Johnson
Riverton, Manitoba

53

Ein er snót með ekkert vamm,
æði langan hala dró.
Hvert eitt spor sem hún gékk fram,
hennar rófa styttist mjó.

. . . . .

There is a lady without reproach
Who pulled a very long tail.
With each step she walked forward,
Her slender tail shortened.

[Solution: sewing needle. - M.E.]

Mrs. Jóhanna Sölvason
Mozart, Saskatchewan

54

Fuglinn flaug fjaðralaus
á vegginn beinlaus,
þá kom maður handalaus
og skaut fuglinn bogalaus.

M.E.: Og þetta er snjórinn og vindurinn?
Jóhanna Thorkelsson: Já.

. . . . .

The bird flew without feathers
Sat down on the wall, boneless,
Then a man came, handless,
And shot the bird, bowless.

M.E: And this is the snow and the wind?
J.Th.: Yes.

Mrs. Jóhanna Thorkelsson
Arnes, Manitoba

55

Fullt hús matar, finnast hvergi dyrnar á. Fimm menn fara um einar dyr, koma þó í sitt herbergi hver.

. . . . .

A house full of food; doors to it cannot be found anywhere. Five men go through the same door, but each enters into a separate room.

[Solution: fingers in a glove. - M.E.]

Mrs. Jóhanna Thorkelsson
Arnes, Manitoba

56

Fundist hefur fram á sjó,
Fjörunni hvergi nærri,
opinmynntur en þögull þó;
þess eru dæmin færri.

. . . . .

Found out on the ocean,
Nowhere near a beach,
Open-mouthed but silent;
Instances of this are few.

[Informant guesses the solution to be: an unmanned boat.]

**Mr. Friðfinnur Lyngdal
Vancouver, British Columbia**

57

>   Gékk ég fyrir hellisdyr,
>   sá ég þar inni lítið laufblað,
>   upp yfir því laufblaði tólf kólfa,
>   upp yfir þeim kólfum tvær vindrifur,
>   upp yfir þeim vindrifum tvö stöðuvötn,
>   upp yfir þeim stöðuvötnum tvo klakka.
>   Svo var yfir háls og hrygg að fara.
>   Kom ég að einu fífuskafti;
>   þar undir er sápustadur.
>   Sá skal í sápustaðinn lenda
>   sem ekki ræður gátuna til enda.

M.E.: Þetta er allt ein gáta?

Jóhanna Thorkelsson: Þetta er allt ein gáta. Veistu hvað það meinar?

M.E.: Nei.

J.Th.: Köttur.

* * * * *

>   I walked before the mouth of the cave,
>   In there I saw a little leaf,
>   Up over the leaf twelve clappers,
>   Up over those clappers two windrifts,
>   Up over those windrifts two lakes,
>   Up over those lakes two saddle hooks.
>   Then one had to travel over hill and ridge.

> I came to a shaft of cotton-grass;
> There under is a place for soap.
> He will end up in the place for soap
> Who doesn't solve the riddle to its end.

M.E.: This is all one riddle?

J.Th.: This is all one riddle. Do you know what it means?

M.E.: No.

J.Th.: A cat.

Mrs. Jóhanna Thorkelsson
Arnes, Manitoba

58

Gékk ég og granni minn,
kona hans og kona mín,
dóttir hans og dóttir mín,
fundum fimm egg í hreiðri,
átum sitt hver og þá var eftir eitt.

Þessir menn voru nágrannar og þeir áttu sína dótturina hver, og það er-- þau voru ekki nema fjögur; þess vegna kom það víst rétt út. Þeir voru giftir dóttur hvers annars.

. . . . .

My neighbor and I went for a walk,
His wife and my wife,
His daughter and my daughter,
Found five eggs in a nest,
Ate one each and yet one remained.

These men were neighbors and they each had a daughter, and that is-- they were only four; that's why it came out right. They were married to each other's daughter.

Mr. Guðmundur Jónasson
Mountain, North Dakota

59

Hvað er útprik og innprik og allra manna prikastik?

˙ ˙ ˙ ˙ ˙

What is an outstick and an instick and everybody's pricklestick?

[Solution: needle. - M.E.]

Mr. Helgi Hornfjörð
Elfros, Saskatchewan

60

Hvað er það sem dettur en brotnar ekki,
fer í sjó og sekkur ekki,
fer í eld en brennur þó?

. . . . .

What is it that falls, but doesn't break,
Goes into the sea and doesn't sink,
But goes into a fire and burns?

[Solution: cork. - M.E.]

Mrs. Jóhanna Thorkelsson
Arnes, Manitoba

61

    Hvað er það sem er í löngum göngum,
    með löngum spöngum,
    gullinu fegra,
    og grípur það enginn?

M.E.: Og það er sólargeislinn?
Jóhanna Thorkelsson: Já.

` ` ` ` `

    What is found in long passageways,
    With long spangles,
    Fairer than gold,
    And no one steals it?

M.E.: And that is the sunbeam?
J.Th: Yes.

                                    Mrs. Jóhanna Thorkelsson
                                    Arnes, Manitoba

62

Hvað er það sem fæðu fær
feikilega neðan í sig?
Upp úr því svo öllu slær.
Er þá gátan breytileg.

. . . . .

What is it that gets food
Exceedingly into itself?
Everything then comes out of it.
The riddle then is changeable.

[Dómhildur Johnson's solution: smoke. Should be: chimney. - M.E.]

Mrs. Dómhildur Johnson
Wynyard, Saskatchewan

63

        Hvað er það sem hoppar og skoppar
        yfir heljarbrú
        með mannabein í maganum?
        Og gettu nú.

Þetta er skip.

        . . . . .

        What is it that hops and skips
        Across the bridge of hell
        With the bones of humans in its belly?
        And, now, guess.

This is a ship.

                                      Mr. Valdimar Johnson
                                      Riverton, Manitoba

64

Hvað hét hundur karls
sem í afdölum bjó?
Nefndi ég hann í fyrsta orði
en þú getur það ekki þó.

. . . . .

What was the name of the old fellow's dog
Who lived in a remote valley?
I named him in the first word
But you still won't guess it.

[Solution: Hvað/= What. - M.E.]

Mrs. Olga Pálsson
Arborg, Manitoba

65

Hver er sá stólpi haglega tilbúinn
sem hefur innyfli af hör eða líni,
klæðnaður allur af kvikfénaði?
Allur er líkaminn á honum dauður,
utan höfuðið einsamalt sem lifir.
Tvær höfuðskepnur tempra honum lífið:
önnur lífgar sál hans,
en önnur hann deyðir.

Þetta þykir mér nú vel sett saman gáta . . . . Það er kerti með ljósi á.

. . . . .

What is that pillar handsomely made
With innards of flax or linen,
All the clothing from livestock?
His whole body is deadExcept the head alone which lives.
Two of the prime elements regulate his life:
One enlivens his soul,
But another deadens him.

Now, this I feel is a well-made riddle . . . . It is a lit candle.

Mr. Gísli Gillis
Wynyard, Saskatchewan

66

Hver er sá veggur víður og hár
vænum skreyttum röndum;
gulur, rauður, grænn og blár,
gerður af meistarans höndum?

Ráðningin er regnboginn.

. . . . .

What is that wall, wide and high,
Decorated with fine stripes;
Yellow, red, green and blue,
Made by the Master's hands?

The solution is the rainbow.

Mr. **Valdimar Johnson**
Riverton, Manitoba

67

Hvert er það hús í heimi,
harla fagurt að líta;
prýtt er það innan með pílunum tólf;
fylgja því tvær og fimmtíu meyjar,
maður og kona af misjöfnum litum?

. . . . .

Which is that house in the world,
Very beautiful to look at,
Decorated inside with twelve spokes;
Two and fifty maidens accompany it,
A man and a woman in dissimilar colours?

[Solution: the year, months, weeks, day and night. - M.E.]

**Mrs. Svava Flanagan
Gardar, North Dakota**

68

Karl skar kú sína á halanum svo af fór höfuđiđ.

Það sýnist vera skrýtið, en það var nefnilega . . . . Hann skar kúna á túnhalanum. [Laughter.]

. . . . .

The old fellow cut his cow on the tail so the head fell off.

It seems strange, but it was, namely . . . . He cut [i.e. slaughtered] the cow on a tail-end of the home-field. [Laughter.]

Mr. Jón Mýrdal
Blaine, Washington

69

Margt er smátt í vettling manns.
Gettu sands [pronounced: sanns]!
Þó þú getir í allan dag,
þá geturðu ekki hans.

. . . . .

There are many small things in a man's mitten.
Guess sand!
Although you guess all day,
You won't get it.

[Solution: sand. - M.E.]

Mr. Valdimar Johnson
Riverton, Manitoba

Riddles

70

Saman bundnir seggir tveir
við saurugt búa;
næturkuldann þola þeir
og þrældóms lúa.

Þetta eru skór.

. . . . .

Two fellows tied together
Live in filth;
They endure the cold of the night
And the weariness of labour.

This is a pair of shoes.

Mr. Valdimar Johnson
Riverton, Manitoba

71

Sat ég og át ég,
og át af mér;
át það ég á sat,
og át af því.

Það var maður sem sat á meri, og hún var að sjúga fol. . . . . . Folald var að sjúga merina. Hann var að borða, og merin var að borða, og folaldið var að drekka.

. . . . .

I sat and ate,
And ate off myself;
Ate what I sat on,
And ate off it.

There was a man who sat on a mare, and she was sucking a foa. . . . . . A foal was sucking at the mare. He was eating, and the mare was eating, and the foal was drinking.

Mrs. Jóhanna Thorkelsson
Arnes, Manitoba

72

Sá ég á veg vega;
vegur var undir
og vegur var yfir
og vegur á alla vegu.

Fugl sem flýgur undir brú.

. . . . .

I saw to the way of ways;
A way was under,
A way was over
And a way in all directions.

A bird flying under a bridge.

Mr. Jón Howardson
Vancouver, British Columbia

73

Sá ég nálarift
næði og láni svift,
fljót fært til ferða lift.
Aldrei fór hún fet,
færðist ekki um set,
stóð þar sem stóllinn hét.
Þó má rekja förin fet
um fatalista tvinna fold
og voð meðan vermir hold.

. . . . .

I saw a lady
Deprived of good fortune and peace,
Quickly lifted for moving.
She never took a step,
Didn't move out of place,
Stood where the chair was,
Still, one can trace her steps
About the land of twine and fashion
And while cloth still warms flesh.

[Solution: floor-model sewing machine. - M.E.]

Mrs. Jóhanna Sölvason
Mozart, Saskatchewan

74

Syfjar mig nú sárlega
svo til gengur árlega,
dauðans bróðir dárlega
dregur að mér fárlega.

. . . . .

Now I feel the need of sleep, sorely,
That's how it goes, annually,
Death's brother, derisively,
Attacks me, feverishly.

[Solution: a hibernating bear. - M.E.]

Sigríður Björnsson
Gimli, Manitoba

75

Tíu toga fjóra,
tvö eru höfuðin á,
rassinn upp og rassinn niður
og rófan aftan á.

. . . . .

Ten pull four,
Two heads on it,
The rump up and the rump down
And the tail behind.

[Solution: a woman milking a cow. - M.E.]

Mrs. Jóhanna Thorkelsson
Arnes, Manitoba

76

Tvíbein sat á þríbein, hélt á einbein. Þá kom fjórbein, tók einbein af tvíbein. Þá reiddist tvíbein, tók þríbein og barði fjórbein, svo fjórbein missti sitt einbein.

Þetta er hundur þegar hann tók beinið af manninum sem var að naga bein.

· · · · ·

Twobone sat on Threebone, held Onebone. Then Fourbone came, took Onebone from Twobone. Then Twobone became angry, took Threebone and hit Fourbone, so Fourbone dropped his Onebone.

This is a dog when he took the bone from the man who was gnawing on a bone.

[Solution: The man was sitting on a three-legged stool. - M. E.]

Mrs. Jóhanna Thorkelsson
Arnes, Manitoba

77

Tvær kindur gengu í garðinn Hvítar;
Önnur var svört en hin var grá.
Hvernig voru þær litar þá?

. . . . .

Two sheep walked into the garden [of] Hvít,
One was black but the other one was gray.
What then were their colours?

[Solution: The name of the owner of the garden was Hvít (= "White"). One of the sheep was black and the other was gray. - M.E.]

Mr. Jón Mýrdal
Blaine, Washington

78

Unknown Man: There it comes.

> Tvær ær gengu í garðinn Hvítar.
> Þó önnur ærin væri grá
> hin var mórauð til að sjá.

> . . . . .

> Two ewes walked into the garden [of] Hvít.
> Although one ewe was gray,
> The other one, seen from afar, was brown.

[Solution: The name of the owner of the garden was Hvít (= "White"). One of the ewes was gray and the other was brown. - M.E.]

Mr. Sigmundur Helgason
Elfros, Saskatchewan

79

Upp ólst bróðir minn hjá mér,
mikið hár á kolli ber.
Í fyrstunni það fallegt erog fagurlega dreifir sér.
En þegar eldist sá,
undarlegt það heita má;
úr honum verður auðargná,
alþakin af hærum grá.
Þessi karlinn sómir sér
sem þó ellimerkin ber,
hárið frá að falla fer,
fölur eftir skallinn er.

Þetta er fífillinn.

. . . . .

My brother grew up with me,
He has much hair on his head.
At first it is so pretty
And spreads itself beautifully.
But, when this one gets older,
Strange it may be called,
From him a rich treasure springs,
Completely covered in gray hairs.
This old fellow carries himself well
Although he bears the marks of age,
The hair begins to fall away,
The pale skull remains.

This is the dandelion.

Mr. Valdimar Johnson
Riverton, Manitoba

80

Þegar ég var í Melgerði, þá gékk ég ofan í nes, sá þar stóran andahóp, skaut strax, drap fjórar. Tvær flugu upp, strax, af þeim, og ein suður í móa. Meðan ég var að elta hana, þá flaug sú sem eftir var.

[* * * *]

Hann skaut fjórar. Tvær flugu upp strax, og ein flaug suður í móa. Þegar hann var að elta hana, þá flaug sú sem eftir var. Hann hefur ekki drepið neina nema þessa einu sem hann elti.

· · · · ·

When I was in Melgerði I walked down to the point, saw there a large flock of ducks, fired right away, killed four. Two of them flew up immediately, and one flew south to the moors. While I was chasing it, the one that remained flew away.

[* * * *]

He shot four. Two flew up immediately, and one flew south to the moors. When he was chasing it, then the one that remained flew away. He hasn't killed any of them except the one he chased.

Mr. Friðfinnur Lyngdal
Vancouver, British Columbia

81

Þegar var fyrir mig gefið gull
gladdi ég margan snauðann;
þegar ég er feit og full
fel ég í mér dauðann.

. . . . .

When gold was given for me
I gladdened many a poor one;
When I am fat and full
I hold death within me.

[Solution: a gun. - M.E.]

Mr. Friðfinnur Lyngdal
Vancouver, British Columbia

Riddles

82

Þessi kerling sómir sér
sem þó ellimerkin ber.
Hárið gráa falla fer,
fölur eftir skallinn er.

. . . . .

This old lady does herself proud
Who, nevertheless, carries the signs of old age.
The gray hair will be falling soon,
The pale, bald head remains.

[Solution: the dandelion. - M.E.]

Valdimar Johnson
Riverton, Manitoba

GAME VERSES

Game Verses 83

> Spáđu mér nú spákona mín
> því sem ég spyr þig ađ,
> og þá skal ég međ gullinu gleđja þig
> og silfrinu seđja þig
> ef þú segir mér satt,
> en í eldinum brenna þig
> ef þú skrökvar ađ mér.

[* * * *]

Þetta er leikur sem viđ gerđum viđ horn, settum völuna á höfuđiđ, svo-- svo spurđum viđ hana einhverja vitleysu, auđvitađ, og-- og þegar viđ vorum búin ađ þilja þetta yfir henni þá teigđum viđ höfuđiđ og þá datt valan á gólfiđ, og þá fór þađ eftir því hvort ađ . . . . En, auđvitađ, brenndum viđ hana aldrei, þó hún segđi okkur ekki alltaf satt.

. . . . .

> Reveal to me my sibyl
> What I ask you,
> And then I will gladden you with gold
> And satisfy you with silver
> If you tell me the truth,
> But burn you in fire
> If you lie to me.

[* * * *]

This was a game we played by a [house] corner, placed the [sheep's] knucklebone on the head, then-- then we asked her some nonsense, of course, and -- and when we had finished reciting this over it, we stretched our necks and then the knucklebone fell to the floor, and then it went according to whether . . . . But, of course, we never burned it, although it didn't always tell us the truth.

Mrs. Hrund Skúlason
Winnipeg, Manitoba

84

> Hann elskar mig
> af öllu hjarta,
> yfirmáta,
> ofurheitt,
> harla lítið,
> og ekki neitt.

Já. There you are.

[* * * *]

Vanalega var það baldursbrá. Það mátti brúka sóley og hvaða blóm sem að var, en mig minnir að baldursbráin væri vanalega notuð því það var svo þægilegt að taka-- tína af henni blöðin.

. . . . .

> He loves me
> With all his heart,
> Exceedingly,
> Very warmly,
> Not much,
> And not at all.

Yes. There you are.

[* * * *]

Usually it was a daisy. You could use a buttercup or whatever flower was at hand, but I seem to remember that the daisy was normally used because it was so easy to take-- pluck off its petals.

Mrs. Hrund Skúlason
Winnipeg, Manitoba

85

Komdu til að kveðast á
karl minn ef þú þorir.
Gjörðu vel við þessa þrjá
það eru landar vorir.

. . . . .

Let's exchange verses
My good fellow, if you dare.
Do well against these three,
They are our compatriots.

Mrs. Sigurveig Sveinsson
Baldur, Manitoba

86

Komdu til að kveðast á
kerling ef þú getur,
láttu ganga ljóðaskrá
lengst í allan vetur.

. . . . .

Let's exchange verses,
Old lady, if you can,
Let flow a catalogue of poems
All through the winter.

                          Mrs. Sigurveig Sveinsson
                          Baldur, Manitoba

RHYMES ABOUT GRÝLA
AND
OTHER SCARY FIGURES

87

Hér er komin Grýla grá eins og örn,
hún er svo vandfædd hún vill ei nema börn.
Hún er svo vandfædd hún vill ei börnin góð,
heldur þau sem hafa miklar hrinur og hljóð,
heldur þau sem löt eru á lestur og söng;
þau eru henni þægilegust þegar hún er svöng.
Þau eru henni þægilegust, það veit ég víst,
ef þau þekktu Grýlu þá gerðu þau það síst.
Ég þekki Grýlu, ég hef hana séð,
hún er bæði ófríð og illileg með.
Hún er svo ófríð að höfuðin ber hún þrjú,
þó er ekkert minna en á miðaldra kú,
þó er ekkert minna, það segja menn,
að hún hafi augnaráðin í hverjum þrenn,
að hún hafi augnaráðin eldsglóðum lík,
kinnabeinin kolgrá og kjaftinn eins og tík.
Kinnabeinin kolgrá og hrútsnefið hátt,
það er í átján hlykkjunum, þrútið og blátt.
Það er í átján hlykkjunum, hárstríið hart,
og ofan fyrir kjaftinn tekur keipótt og svart.
Ofan fyrir hökur taka tennurnar tvær.

Nú. [Pause.]

Eyrun hanga, sex saman, sitt ofan á lær,
eyrun hanga, sex saman, selgrá á lit.
Hökuskeggið, hæruskotið, heilfullt af nyt,

hökuskeggið, hæruskotið, höndurnar þá,
stórar eins og kálfskló og kartnöglur á.

Ég held ég kunni ekki meira.

. . . . .

Here Grýla has arrived, gray as an eagle,
She is so particular about food, she only wants children.
She is so particular about food, she doesn't want good children,
Rather those that make great howls and noises,
Rather those who are lazy at reading and song;
They are the most convenient for her, when she is hungry.
They are the most convenient for her, that I know,
If they knew Grýla they would be less likely to carry on.
I know Grýla, I have seen her,
She is both ugly and evil-looking.
She is so ugly that she has three heads,
Yet none is smaller than that on a middle-aged cow,
Yet nothing is smaller, and that men do say,
That she has eyes in each of the three,
That she has eyes like glowing embers,
Dark gray cheekbones and a mouth like a bitch,
Dark gray cheekbones and a ram's nose high,
It's in eighteen bumps, swollen and blue,
It's in eighteen bumps. The coarse, straw-like hair,
Reaches below the mouth, freaky and black.
Two teeth descend below her chins.

Now. [Pause.]

Six ears hang together each down to a thigh,
Six ears hang together of seal-gray colour.

The grizzled chin beard, full of vermin,
The grizzled chin beard, then the hands,
Large as calf's claws with thickened nails.

I don't think I know any more of it.

Mr. Hjörtur Hjartarson
Lundar, Manitoba

88

    Kerling heitir Grýla,
    hún er grá og loðin.
    Horn hefur hún úr hausi,

(Það er nú ekki fallegt, "úr hausi"!)

    álnalangt að kalla.
    Tönnur hefur hún stórar,
    þær ná ofan á bringu.
    Tungan er ljót og leið,
    og loðin er svo skrokkur.

(<u>Oh, I think I have forgotten</u>.)

    Hún stendur í horni
    þar sem börnin stafa,
    ef þau æpa og hrína
    og nenna ekki að lesa
    þá kemur gráa Grýla
    og grípur þau í poka.
    Hún flytur þau til fjalla,
    fer þá mikið illa.
    Ef þau iðni stunda,
    eru þekk og hlýðin,
    kemur aldrei Grýla,
    því hún vill ekki góð börn.

Þetta er allt.

. . . . .

    An old crone is called Grýla,
    She is gray and shaggy.

Rhymes About Grýla and Other Scary Figures

She has horns on her head,

(That really isn't nice, "on her noggin"!)

The length of an ell, might be said.
She has large teeth,
They reach down to her chest.
The tongue is long and ugly,
And the body is hairy.

(Oh, I think I have forgotten.)

She stands in the corner
Where the children are spelling.
If they howl and whine
And are too lazy to read,
Then Grýla comes
And grabs them for her poke.
She takes them to the mountains
Where bad things happen.
If they apply themselves diligently,
Are well-behaved and obedient,
Grýla will never come
Because she doesn't want good children.

That's all.

Mrs. Þórey Björnsson
Mountain, North Dakota

89

    Kom ég út og kerling leit ófrýna,
    kátlega hún á mig tók að blína.
    Spurði ég hana um heitanafngift sína.
    „Hér er, " segir hún, „Grýla, skrítin trýna.
    Börnin þau sem hrekkjótt eru og hrína,
    best mun vera í pokann minn að tína.
    Sesselja, sem sjaldan lætur dvína,
    seldu me. .-- seldu mér hana keipaskjóðu þína."
    – „Farðu burtu flagðið þitt til svína,
    þú færð hana aldrei, litlu dóttur mína."

Þetta er Grýluvísa.

    . . . . .

    I came out and saw a frowning crone,
    Gleefully she began staring at me.
    I asked her about her name.
    "Here is," she says, "Grýla, strange of snout.
    The children who are wicked and whine
    Would be best to tuck into my poke.
    Sesselja, who seldom lets up,
    Sell m. .-- sell me your fretful one."
    – "Go away you hag, to the swine!
    You will never get my little daughter."

This is a Grýla verse.

Mrs. Jóhanna Thorkelsson
Arnes, Manitoba

Rhymes About Grýla and Other Scary Figures

90*

Ekki linnir umferðinni um Fljótsdalinn enn,
mér er sagt að þar búi þrifnaðar –
mér er sagt að þar búi þrifnaðarmenn.
Hér er komin Grýla sem getur enginn satt,
hún er svo vandfædd hún vill ei börnin góð,
heldur þau sem gefa af sér hrinur,
já, heldur þau sem gefa af sér hrinur og hljóð.

. . . . .

The traffic through Fljótsdal still doesn't let up,
I am told that there dwell prosperous,
I am told that there dwell prosperous men.
Grýla has arrived here whom none can satisfy,
She is so difficult to feed, she doesn't want the good children,
Rather those who give off howls,
Yes, rather those who give off howls and bellows.

Miss Margrét Bjarnason
Arborg, Manitoba

---

* See music transcription for this item on page 301.

91

Grýla reið fyrir ofan garð,
hafði hala fimmtán,
en í hverjum hala hundrað belgi,
en í hverjum belg, börn tuttugu.
Þar vantaði á eitt;
þar skal fara í barnið leitt:
hún Sigga!

. . . . .

Grýla rode beyond the wall,
Had fifteen tails,
But in each tail a hundred bellies,
But in each belly twenty children.
One was still lacking;
A tiresome child will go there:
That will be Sigga!

Mrs. Sigríður Björnsson
Gimli, Manitoba

92

        Grýla reið með garði
        gékk með henni Varði.
        Dró hún belg með læri,
        börn trúi ég í væru. [Laughter.]
        Litla-- litla Sigga hljóp þar út,
        hafði upp í sér snæri,
        tók hún band og hnýtti af hnút,
        hleypti öllum börnum út,
        svo trúi ég þetta væri. [Laughter.]

Þetta er meiri vitleysan.

        . . . . .

        Grýla rode along the wall,
        Varði walked with her.
        She pulled a bag alongside her thigh;
        I believe that in it were children. [Laughter.]
        Little-- little Sigga ran out,
        Had a piece of string in her mouth,
        She took the cord and untied the knot,
        Let all the children out.
        That's how I believe it was. [Laughter.]

What a lot of nonsense.

                      Mrs. Frída Holm
                      Vancouver, British Columbia

93

Hér er komin Grýla og gægist um hól,
hún ætlar að hvíla sig hér um öll jól.
Hún ætlar að hvíla sig, því hana vantar börn,
hún er grá um hálsinn og hlakkar eins og örn.
Hún er grá um hálsinn og hleypur út í fjós,
hún vill ekki horfa í það hátíðaljós.
Hún vill ekki heyra þann hátíðasöng,
kvartar hún um ketleysi og kveðst vera svöng.
Kvartar hún um ketleysi, kjökrandi þá:
„Ég vil fá mér barnkorn í belginn minn grá.
Ég vil fá mér barnkorn sem belja og hrína kann,
mér er sagt hann Magnús litli syngi sönginn þann.
Mér er sagt hann Magnús litli hljóðar og hrín,
komdu þá í belginn minn barnkindin mín."

. . . . .

Grýla has arrived here and peeks around the knoll,
She is going to rest here through all of yule.
She is going to rest, because she needs children,
She is gray about the neck and screams like an eagle.
She is gray about the neck and runs out to the byre;
She doesn't want to look at that festive light.
She doesn't want to hear that festive song,
She complains about the lack of meat and claims she is hungry.
She complains about the lack of meat, whimpering so:
"I want to get a child into my gray belly.
I want to get a child who can bellow and whine,

I am told that little Magnús sings that song.
I am told that little Magnús bellows and whines,
Come then into my belly my little child."

Mrs. Sigríður Björnsson
Gimli, Manitoba

94

Grýla kallar á börnin sín
þegar hún fer að sjóða til jóla.
„Komið þið hingað öll til mín,
ykkur vil ég bjóða:
Leppur, Skreppur,
Lápur, Skrápur,
Langleggur og leiðinda Skjóða,
Völustallur og Bóla,
Sigurður og Sóla."

. . . . .

Grýla calls her children
When she starts cooking for yule.
"Come to me, here, all of you,
I wish to invite you:
Leppur, Skreppur,
Lápur, Skrápur,
Langleggur and tiresome Skjóða,
Völustallur and Bóla,
Sigurður and Sóla.

Mrs. Sigríður Björnsson
Gimli, Manitoba

95

Það á að gefa börnum brauð
að bíta í á jólunum,
kertaljós og klæðin rauð
svo komist þau úr bólunum,
væna flís af feitum sauð
sem fjakka-- fjalla gékk á hólunum.
Nú er hún gamla Grýla dauð,
gafst hún upp á rólunum.

. . . . .

Children should be given bread
To bite into at yuletide,
Candlelight and red garments
So they can get out of their beds,
A good piece off a fat sheep
That fjakka-- grazed the mountain knolls.
Now old Grýla is dead;
She gave up on her wanderings.

Mrs. Sigríður Björnsson
Gimli, Manitoba

96

Við skulum ekki hafa hátt,
hér er margt að ugga.
Ég hef heyrt í alla nótt
andardrátt á glugga.

· · · · ·

Let us be very quiet,
Here there are many things to fear.
I have heard all night long,
Breathing at the window.

                    Mrs. Sigríður Björnsson
                    Gimli, Manitoba

97

Við skulum ekki hafa hátt,
hér er maður á glugganum.
Hann er vanur að henda smátt
og hylja sig í skugganum.

. . . . .

Let us be very quiet,
There is a man at the window.
He is used to watching many a thing
And hiding in the shadow.

                                          Mrs. Sigríður Björnsson
                                          Gimli, Manitoba

98

Haf þú ekki hátt um þig
hér er kominn maður,
nýbúinn að næra sig
nógu hress og glaður.

. . . . .

Don't carry on loudly,
A man has arrived here,
He has recently eaten,
Is happy and in good spirits.

Mrs. Sigríður Björnsson
Gimli, Manitoba

99

Hér er kominn Dúðadurtur,
digur bæði og hár,
bíður fram í bæjardyrum,
bröndóttur og grár.

. . . . .

Dúðadurtur has arrived here,
Both portly and tall,
He waits by the outside door,
Brindled and gray.

Mrs. Sigríður Björnsson
Gimli, Manitoba

LULLABIES AND SOOTHERS

100

Bí, bí og blaka,
álftirnar kvaka,
ég læt sem ég sofi
en samt mun ég vaka.

. . . . .

Bí, bí and flutter by
The swans are calling,
I pretend I'm sleeping,
But, even so, I'll be awake.

Mr. Kár Simundson
Arborg, Manitoba

101

Ég skal kveđa viđ þig vel,
viljir þú hlýđa barnkind mín.
Pabbi þinn er ađ sækja sel,
ađ sjóđa fer hún móđir þín.

. . . . .

I will sing for you, well,
If you are attentive, my child.
Your papa went to fetch a seal;
Your mother will soon start cooking.

**Mrs. Sigríđur Björnsson
Gimli, Manitoba**

102

Farđu ađ sofa fyrir mig
fyrst þú mátt og getur,
ég skal breiđa ofan á þig
ofurlítiđ betur.

. . . . .

Go to sleep for me
Since you may and are able,
I will cover you up
Just a little better.

Mrs. Sigríđur Björnsson
Gimli, Manitoba

103

Farðu að lúra og liggja og kúra,
lambið góða mitt,
mjólkin súra, milli dúra,
mettir brjóstið þitt.

. . . . .

Go to bed and doze and nuzzle
My good lamb,
The sour milk, between naps,
Will satiate your breast.

Mr. Waldimar Johnson
Wynyard, Saskatchewan

104

Lambið og ljúfan
og líneikin fín,
dyggðanna dúfan
dóttir góð mín.

. . . . .

A lamb and a love
And a lady fine,
A dove of virtues,
My good daughter.

                        Mr. Þórður Bjarnason
                        Gimli, Manitoba

105

Hættu að hrína Mangi minn
á morgunn kemur skipið;
færir þér hann faðir þinn
fíkjurnar og sykurinn.
Ekki kemur Hjaltalín með hripið.

. . . . .

Quit your blubbering, dear Mangi,
Tomorrow the ship comes.
Your father will bring you
Figs and sugar.
Hjaltalín still hasn't brought the crib-box.

Mrs. Sigríður Björnsson
Gimli, Manitoba

PRAYER VERSES

106

Nú er ég klæddur, kominn á ról,
Kristur Jesú veri mitt skjól.
Í guðsóttanum gefðu mér,
að ganga í dag svo líki þér.

. . . . .

Now I am dressed, up and about,
Christ Jesus be my refuge.
In fear of God, allow me
To go about this day in likeness of you.

Mrs. Helga Howardson
Vancouver, British Columbia

107

Ég man eftir einu versi sem að ég held að faðir minn hafi nú-- kenndi mér fremur, og það var þar sem hann girti yfir rúmið fyrir-- þegar hann var barn, fyrir draugum og djöflum.

M.E.: Já. Farðu með það.

> Vertu yfir og allt um kring
> með eilífri blessun þinni;
> Sitji guðs englar saman í hring
> sænginni yfir minni.

Þá var komin girðing utan um rúmið til þess að fjandinn [laughter] gæti ekki komið, að minnsta kosti. Þá kemur trúin til greina. Það trúði þessu; þetta væri vö rnin, að þetta illa, hvað sem það héti (hvort það væri nú persóna-- höfuð-persónan sjálf, eða eitthvað annað) að þá væri vörn í þessu.

. . . . .

I remember one prayer that I think my father had-- taught me, rather, and that was where he fenced in the bed-- when he was a child, against spooks and devils.

M.E.: Yes. Recite that.

> Be over and all around
> With Your eternal blessing;
> God's angels, together, sit in a circle
> Over my bed.

Prayer Verses 173

A fence was thus made around the bed so that the Devil [laughter] couldn't come near, at least. This is where belief comes in. They believed this, that this was the protection. That this evil (whatever it was called, whether it was a person-- the Head Personage himself, or something else)-- that there was protection in this.

Mr. Björn Bjarnason
Arborg, Manitoba

108

Leggðu þína líknarhönd
á líkama bæði og mína önd,
en seinast þegar ég sofna fer
setjist guðs englar yfir mér.

. . . . .

Lay your healing hand
On my body and spirit,
And when at last I go to sleep
God's angels sit over me.

Mrs. Sigríður Björnsson
Gimli, Manitoba

109

Nú til hvíldar halla ég mér
höfgi að augum síga fer.
Alskyggn drottinn, augu þín
yfir vaki hvílu mín.

. . . . .

Now I lie down to rest,
Drowsiness settles over my eyes.
All-seeing Lord, may your eyes
Watch over my bed.

Mrs. Sigurveig Sveinsson
Baldur, Manitoba

110

Drottinn láttu mig dreyma vel
sem dyggan Jakob Ísrael.
Þegar á steini sætt hann svaf
sæla værð honum náð þín gaf.

. . . . .

Lord let me dream well
As faithful Jakob of Israel.
When on the stone he sweetly slept
Your grace gave him blissful sleep.

**Sigríður Björnsson
Gimli, Manitoba**

111

Blessuð sólin skín á skjá
skær með ljóma sínum.
Herra Jesú himnum á
hjálpa mér frá pínu.

. . . . .

The blessed sun shines on the window
With its bright radiance.
Lord Jesus in Heaven
Save me from affliction.

                                            Sigurveig Sveinsson
                                                Baldur, Manitoba

112

Gott er að treysta guð á þig,
gleður það mannsins hjarta.
Yfirgefðu aldrei mig
englaljósið bjarta.

. . . . .

It is good to trust in you, God,
It gladdens a man's heart.
Never abandon me
Bright angel-light.

Sigurveig Sveinsson
Baldur, Manitoba

DRINKING SONGS

Drinking Songs

113*

Gleði raskast, vantar vín;
verður brask að gera,
ef að taskan opnast mín
á þar flaska að vera.

. . . . .

Joy fails, wine is needed;
Measures have to be taken,
If my valise opens
There should be a bottle there.

Mr. Páll Hallson
Winnipeg, Manitoba

---

* See music transcription for this item on page 302.

114*

Ég fór á stað með fullan kút
og fannst ei vert að spara.
Meyjan veifaði vasaklút
og vildi með mér fara.

Þetta er gott. [Laughter.]

. . . . .

I set out with a full keg
And didn't think it necessary to be sparing.
The maiden waved a handkerchief
And wanted to go with me.

That's good. [Laughter.]

Mrs. Jóhanna Thorkelsson
Arnes, Manitoba

---

* See music transcription for this item on page 302.

Drinking Songs

115*

Nú er hlátur nývakinn;
nú er grátur tregur;
nú er ég kátur nafni minn;
nú er ég mátulegur.

. . . . .

Now laughter is newly awakened;
Now weeping is scarce;
Now I am merry, dear namesake;
Now I am just right.

Mr. Páll Hallson
Winnipeg, Manitoba

---

* See music transcription for this item on page 303.

116*

Hér er ekkert hrafnaþing;
hér er enginn tregi.
Farðu vel með Vatnsdæling,
vinur elskulegi.

. . . . .

This is no gathering of ravens;
Here there is no sadness.
Treat well this man of Vatnsdal,
Dear friend.

Mr. Björn Bjarnason
Arborg, Manitoba

---

* See music transcription for this item on page 303.

Drinking Songs

117*

Þetta er það sem við Tími gamli fórum stundum með:

> Bakkus sjóli sæll við bikar
> situr á stóli tignar hám.
> Eins og sólin öðling blikar
> upp í jólna sölum blám.

. . . . .

This is what old Tími and I used to sing:

> King Bakkus happy at drink
> Sits on a chair of high rank.
> The noble fellow twinkles like the sun
> Up in the blue halls of the gods.

Mr. Björn Bjarnason
Arborg, Manitoba

---

* See music transcription for this item on page 304.

118*

Ekki á ég kýr og ekki á ég ær
Og ekkert skylt við ríka;
fullur í dag og fullur í gær,
og fullur á morgun líka.

· · · · ·

I don't have cows and I don't have ewes
And nothing in common with the wealthy;
Drunk today and drunk yesterday,
And also drunk tomorrow.

Mrs. Jóhanna Thorkelsson
Arnes, Manitoba

---

* See music transcription for this item on page 304.

Drinking Songs

119*

Illt er mér í augunum,
eru það syndagjöldin.
Dágott þykir draugunum
að drollast heim á kvöldin.

. . . . .

My eyes ache,
That is the payment for my sins.
Sluggards really like
Dragging themselves home late at night.

Mr. Tímoteus Böðvarsson
Gimli, Manitoba

---

* See music transcription for this item on page 305.

DANCES AND REELS

Dances and Reels

120*

Hjartað af ánægju hlær í mér
hvenær sem kvissi-vals nefndur er.
Hoppa ég þá bæði á hæli og tá
og hringsólast reikandi til og frá.

    Refrain: Því að ég enn er frá á fæti
                   fer ég á dans því ég elska rall.
                   Heila nótt ég hoppað gæti.
                   Húrra! Nú ætti að verða ball.

Dansið þið meyjar og dansið þið fljóð,
dansið á jólunum börnin góð.
Dansið þið kóngar og kotungar
og kaupmenn, sjómenn og borgarar.

    Refrain: Meðan ég enn er frá á fæti
                   fer ég í dans því ég elska rall.
                   Heila nótt ég hoppað gæti.
                   Húrra! Því nú á að verða ball.

Dansinn höfum við Danskinum frá;
Danskurinn gaf okkur stjórnarskrá.
Margt hefur Danskurinn vel oss veitt
þó viljum við kannast það lítið eitt.

    Refrain: Meðan ég enn er frá á fæti
                   fer ég í dans því ég elska rall.
                   Heila nótt ég hoppa af kæti.
                   Húrra! Því nú á að verða ball.

Þetta er gott. Þetta er búið.

                   . . . . .

---

* See music transcription for this item on page 306.

My heart laughs with pleasure
Whenever the whisper-waltz is mentioned.
Then I hop both on heel and toe
And dizzily circle to and fro.

>Refrain: Because I'm still light on my feet,
>I go to a dance because I love a good time.
>I could hop about the whole night.
>Hurrah! Now there should be a dance.

Dance you maidens and dance you ladies,
Dance at yule my good children.
Dance you kings and cottagers,
And merchants, seamen and city folk.

>Refrain: While I am still light on my feet,
>I go to a dance because I love a good time.
>I could hop about the whole night.
>Hurrah! Because now there is going to be a dance.

The dance we have from the Danisher.
The Danisher gave us a constitution.
Many good things the Danish have done for us,
Although we don't much want to admit it.

>Refrain: While I am still light on my feet
>I go to a dance because I love a good time.
>I hop with joy the whole night through.
>Hurrah! Because now there is going to be a dance.

This is fine. This is finished.

Mrs. Jóhanna Thorkelsson
Arnes, Manitoba

121*

Í hálfan annan mánuð hef ég hugsað um
hvað það er hérna dauft á Sandinum,
en af því að ég er ungur og ekki laus við rall,
þá ætla ég að stinga upp á að hafa grímuball.
En konur mega ekki koma þar,
sem kannske eru nýgiftar,
og ekki heldur ungmeyjar
sem öðrum eru lofaðar;
þær geta máske girnst í margar grímurnar.

. . . . .

For a month and a half I've thought about
How dull it is here on the Sandur,
But because I am young, and not free of fun,
I'm going to suggest we have a masked ball.
But ladies won't be allowed there
Who perhaps are newly wed,
And not young maidens either
Who are promised to others;
They might be tempted by many of the masks.

Mr. Andrés Guðbjartsson
Hnausa, Manitoba

---

* See music transcription for this item on page 307.

122*

En það var vísa þarna frá Patreksfirði un Ólaf nokkurn Indriðason.

> Í æskunnar indæla blóma,
> ég, Ólafur Indriðason,
> læðist burt frá leiðinda dróma;
> ég lifi í þér indæla von.
> Það uppljómar allt í sinni línu
> ef að eina ég fengi hana Stínu,
> að dansa við það dyggðaríka sprund.
> Það dregur hroll og böl úr minni lund,
> og bætir mein og böl,
>   og bætir mein og böl.

. . . . .

But there was a verse from Patreksfjörður, about a certain Ólafur Indriðason.

> In the delightful bloom of youth,
> I, Ólafur Indriðason,
> Steal away from the fetters of boredom;
> I live in you, lovely hope.
> It brightens everything up
> If I got Stína, by herself,
> To dance with that maiden rich in virtue.
> It draws chill and misery from my mind,
> And heals woe and misery,
>   And heals woe and misery.

Mr. Andrés Guðbjartsson
Hnausa, Manitoba

---

* See music transcription for this item on page 308.

123

Suður í Hafnarfjörð ég flý
og fer í kenderí,
því fjörđurinn er alltaf okkar fyrirheitna land,
því fólk kemst oft, í bílunum, í trúlofunarstand.
Þótt ökutækin ónýt sé og yfirfull af skríl,
þá leynist stundum lagleg stúlka í ljótum kassabíl.
Ó yngismær, ef þú una vilt hjá mér,
þá leigi ég mér lúxusbíl og líð á burt með þér.

. . . . .

I flee south to Hafnarfjörður
And go on a toot,
Because the Fjörđur is always our Promised Land,
Because, on the buses, people often get in an engagement mode.
Although the vehicles are run down and full of rabble,
Sometimes a pretty girl is hidden away in an ugly box-car.
Oh young maiden, if you would abide with me,
I will rent a posh automobile and glide off with you.

Mr. Hjörtur Hjartarson
Lundar, Manitoba

124

Á ég að hryggjast eða gleðjast
eða reiðast mær,
af því að úr augum þínum
ástin til mín hlær.

Á ég að hlæja eða gráta,
af því litla mey,
að þú virðist vilja státa
og við mig segja, „nei."

. . . . .

Should I become sad or glad
Or angry, girl,
Because from your eyes
Love smiles to me.

Should I laugh or cry,
Because, young girl,
You seem to want to challenge me
And tell me, "No."

Mr. Gunnlaugur Holm
Vancouver, British Columbia

Dances and Reels

125*

„Svo er nú komið, systir mín,
sannlega væri það gæfan þín,
að yfirgæfirðu hann Andersen
og þú fengir hann Pedersen."

„Víst er þetta sem þú segir,
sannlega væri það heillaráð.
Ég vildi að guð minn góður gæfi
að gæti ég í kokkinn náð."

. . . . .

"The way it is, my sister,
It would truly be your good fortune
If you dropped that Andersen
And took up with Pedersen."

"What you say is true,
It would surely be good advice.
I'd really like it if good God granted
That I could nab the cook."

Mr. Andrés Guðbjartsson
Hnausa, Manitoba

---

* See music transcription for this item on page 309.

126*

Hann bað mín um daginn hann Bjössi á Hól.
Hann bauð að gefa mér silkikjól,
allskonar léreft of undur fín
er ágæt væru í rykkilín,
og silfurbelti og sumarskó,
og sjálegt albúm frá Jóni hó,
alls konar slifsi og einkaskrín
ef yrði ég konan sín.
Hann Bjössi, hann Bjössi,
hann var svo skotinn ég hræddist hann sjá.
Hann Bjössi, hann Bjössi,
Því hvíslaði ég að honum, „já."

. . . . .

Bjössi from Hóll proposed to me the other day.
He offered to give me a silk dress,
All kinds of linen and wonders fine
That would be good enough for a surplice,
And a silver belt and summer shoes
And a handsome album from Jón Hó,
All kinds of scarves and a notions box
If I became his wife.
That Bjössi, that Bjössi,
He was so smitten I was afraid to look at him.
That Bjössi, that Bjössi,
Because of that I whispered to him, "Yes."

Mrs. Þórunn Anderson
Gimli, Manitoba

---

* See music transcription for this item on page 310.

127*

Sjáið þið sigluna svigna!
Nú gengur það glatt,
ég segi það satt,
ég vildi að hann vildi ekki ligna.
Svo uni ég mér
aleinn hjá þér,
og stundum með annarri hendi vil halda,
en hinni ég sveifla yfir mittið á þér,
og kyssi þig blítt meðan klýf sundur alda.
Nú krafta ég finn,
sem aldrei hef vitað að voru hjá mér.

. . . . .

See the mast swaying!
Now it goes merrily,
I tell the truth,
I wish it wouldn't let up.
Then I'll be content,
Alone with you,
And sometimes steer with one hand,
But the other I throw about your waist
And kiss you tenderly while the wave parts.
I now find powers
That I never knew I possessed.

Mr. Valdimar Johnson
Riverton, Manitoba

---

* See music transcription for this item on page 311.

128*

Hann Lalli minn er laglegur á kinn,
    er laglegur á kinn.
Labbar og fellur ljúfurinn
og lærir undir skólann sinn.
Hann Lalli minn er laglegur á kinn,
    er laglegur á kinn.

Hún Ann, Ann, Ann, sem allar listir kann,
    sem allar listir kann,
einhverntíma eignast mann
og hann gerir farsælan.
Hún Ann, Ann, Ann sem allar listir kann,
    sem allar listir kann.

Hún Trín, Trín, Trín, hún er svo skolli fín,
    hún er svo skolli fín.
Eitt um bið ég auðalín.
Aldrei held ég hún verði mín,
hún Trín, Trín, Trín, hún er svo skolli fín,
    hún er svo skolli fín.

. . . . .

That dear Lalli is fair of cheek,
    Is fair of cheek.
The dear walks and stumbles
And studies for school.
That dear Lalli is fair of cheek,
    Is fair of cheek.

---

* See music transcription for this item on page 312.

That Ann, Ann, Ann who knows all the arts,
    Who knows all the arts,
Will someday have a husband
And make him happy.
That Ann, Ann, Ann who knows all the arts,
    Who knows all the arts.

That Trín, Trín, Trín, she is so very fine,
    She is so very fine.
One thing I ask the maiden.
I don't think she will ever be mine.
That Trín, Trín, Trín, she is so very fine,
    She is so very fine.

Mrs. Sigrídur Björnsson
Gimli, Manitoba

129*

Týri minn og Týri minn,
til hvers ert þú kominn?
   – Til að fá mér meyjarkoss.
Þú mátt fara,
   þú mátt fara,
þér er brugðin vonin;
þetta færðu ekki hnoss.

Það er svona stundum,
   það er svona stundum.
Það er valt að treysta sprundum.
Það er svona stundum,
   það er svona stundum.
Það er aldrei nema kross.

. . . . .

Dear Týri and dear Týri,
Why have you come?
   – To get me a maiden's kiss.
You may go,
   You may go,
Your hope fails you;
This treasure you won't get.

That's sometimes the way it is,
   That's sometimes the way it is.
It's risky to trust women.
That's sometimes the way it is,
   That's sometimes the way it is.
It's never anything but a cross.

Mrs. Guðrún Magnússon
Arborg, Manitoba

---

* See music transcription for this item on page 312.

Dances and Reels

130*

Hann Siggi litli á sólunum,
    á sólunum, á sólunum,
hann er stimamjúkur við stúlkurnar,
en strandaglópur í ástum.
Hann sagði, „Elsku Gunna mín,
    Gunna mín, Gunna mín,
tal um ástina, elskan mín,
er um að gera í næði." [Laughter.]

. . . . .

Little Siggi on his soles,
    On his soles, on his soles,
He's accommodating to the girls,
But in love affairs always left behind.
He said, "Darling Gunna mine,
    Gunna mine, Gunna mine,
Talk about love, my darling,
Is best done in private." [Laughter.]

Mrs. Þórunn Anderson
Gimli, Manitoba

---

* See music transcription for this item on page 313.

HUMOUR AND SATIRE

131

Séð hef ég margt um sögufrón
sérlegt að mínum dómi.
Mig dreymdi að leit ég spón,
mat vel og hana í tómi.
Best var vörin þessi slétt,
þar stóð á skaftið grafið nett:
R-J-Ó-M-I. [Laughter.]

. . . . .

I have seen a lot about the land of the sagas,
Very unique in my judgement.
I dreamt I beheld a spoon,
Appraised it carefully at leisure.
The best part was its smooth lip,
There on the handle, neatly carved, it said:
C-R-E-A-M. [Laughter.]

Mr. Valdimar Johnson
Riverton, Manitoba

132*

Einn réri út á báti,
Ingjaldur í skinnfeldi;
brenglaði átján önglum,
Ingjaldur í skinnfeldi.
Hann kom aldrei aftur,
Ingjaldur í skinnfeldi.

. . . . .

Alone he rowed out in a boat,
Ingjaldur in a skin coat.
He jumbled up eighteen hooks,
Ingjaldur in a skin coat.
He never returned,
Ingjaldur in a skin coat.

                      Mrs. Ingibjörg Bjarnason
                      Gimli, Manitoba

---

* See music transcription for this item on page 313.

Humour and Satire

133*

Hann Árni er látinn í Leiru
og lagður í ískalda mold,
horfinn frá sulti og seyru
því sálin er skilin við hold.

Úr heimi er formaður farinn
sem frameftir ævinni svaf.
Nú grætur þöngull og þarinn
því Árni er pillaður af.

. . . . .

Árni of Leira has passed away
And is laid out in ice-cold earth,
Gone from hunger and starvation
Because the soul has parted from flesh.

A foreman has gone from the world
Who slept through much of his life.
Now weeps the tangle and sea-weed
Because Árni has been dispatched.

Mr. Björn Bjarnason
Arborg, Manitoba

---

* See music transcription for this item on page 314.

134

Hvar býr Nípa?
    – Fyrir ofan garð.
Hvað gerir hún þar?
    – Verpir eggjum.
Mörgum á dag?
    – Mælir fullan. [Laughter.]
Hvað gefur hún gestum?
    – Graut og flautir.
Hvað gefur hún prestum?
    – Skyr og rjóma.
En hvað gefur hún mér?
    – Allt það sem úti frýs
    og ekki kemur í paradís.
    Það er bæði maðkur og mýs,
    mannaskítur og færilýs. [Laughter.]

M.E.: Farðu með hana einu sinni enn.
Jón Howardson: Ég hef orðið mér til skammar. [Laughter.] Ég ætti að hætta.

· · · · ·

Where does Nípa dwell?
    – Beyond the garden wall.
What does she do there?
    – Lays eggs.
Many a day?
    – A full measure.
What does she offer her guests?
    – Pudding and whipped milk.
What does she offer priests?
    – Yoghurt and cream.

> But what does she offer me?
>   Everything outside that freezes,
>   And won't enter paradise.
>   That is, both worms and mice,
>   Human waste and lice. [Laughter.]

M.E.: Recite it once more.
J.H.: I have embarrassed myself. [Laughter.] I should quit.

Mr. Jón Howardson
Vancouver, British Columbia

135

Þegar Halldóra bekkinn braut
bomsa náði í henni.
Gyðjan ofan á gólfið hraut,
glöggt þann atburð kenni.
Salvör í Króki sat þar hjá
sú var berygld í framan.
Halldóra litum bústin brá
bískældist hún öll saman;
Það þótti þegnum gaman.

. . . . .

When Halldóra broke the bench
She made a bang.
The goddess fell to the floor,
I remember the incident clearly.
Salvör of Krókur sat close by,
Her face was all contorted.
Chubby Halldóra changed colours,
And made faces;
Everyone thought that was funny.

Mrs. Jóhanna Thorkelsson
Arnes, Manitoba

NARRATIVE POEMS

136*

Forðum tíðar ríkti í Róm
ræsir einn á láði,
kristnum veitti dauðadóm,
drottins vini þjáði,
fjöri svifti frá.
Díokletianus er
argur nefndur sá.
Ótal marga helga hér
í Helitisses lá.

Þar til setti þengill mann
þessa iðju að hafa,
Sinforíanus heitir hann,
hér um bækur skrafa.
Son einn átti sá.
Einhvern dag sem um er tjéð
út gékk borðum frá,
síðan fékk á foldu séð
fagra baugagná.

Agnes hét sú öðla mær
ára fjórtán talin,
dáfríð mjög og dyggðin skær
af drottini þar til valin
honum að þjóna þrátt.
Á bænagjörðum brúðurin var
bæði dag og nótt.

* See music transcription for this item on page 314.

Heilagar offrur hún fram bar,
um heiðna gaf sig fátt.

Sinfóríanus sonur þá
seima lítur hildi,
vel líst honum auðgrund á
eiga fljóðið vildi,
bónorð byrja fer.
Vildi ei líta heiðinn hal
hún sem tryggðir ber.
Við hann síðan vék á tal:
„Víktu burt frá mér."

Hugarkvöl og harðaböl,
heim gengur til borgar,
dauðsjúkur af ástaröl.
Það aflaði honum sorgar,
hann fékk ei unga frú.
Sínum föður segja vann
satt frá þessu nú.
Sinfóríanus sendi mann
seims að tala við frú.

Elskhuga kvaðst hún eiga sér
ei því giftast vildi.
„Trúlofuð til ekta ég er
annan því ei skildi
heims aðhallast mann.
Minn brúðgumi," mælti víf,
„meyjarson er hann.
Ég skal meðan endist líf
elska af hjarta þann.

„Hans er morgungáfan góð

gæska sem ei dvínar.
Hans rauðleita rósablóð
rjóði á varir mínar;
mjólk og hunang með.
Svoddan kreddi mettar mig
mitt svo hressist geð.
Hann lét af elsku sjálfan sig
særa og negla á tréð.

Hann og líka æðstur er
allra veraldar manna.
Ómögulegt er ykkur mér
yndi hans að banna;
það treysti ég eflaus á.
Enginn hlutur heims um byggð
honum mig skilur frá.
Ann ég honum af allri tryggð
sem alrei þrjóta má."

Síðan kemur sendur heim
segir allt af létta.
Sinfóríanus svarar þeim,
að sig kvað undra þetta,
að sjá hvað heimsk hún er.
„Hver mun sjá í kappa krans,
sem kæran ætlar sér,
þar ég er æðstur innan lands
og minn sonur hér."

Heiðinn einn sem hermdi frá
honum gegndi fyrstur:
„Er það enginn efi á,
er það Jesús Kristur

sem hún eignar sér.
Forlegt hefur Mahómet
menn sem tigna hér.
Þvílík villa, þess ég get,
þykir skaði mér."

Heiðnum konum hér við brá
hofinu sem þéna,
þær lofuðu guð með gullauðs gná
og gerðu ei hljóðin réna.
Hljóm svo hvellan bar.
Var þá glæpugt goðahús
guðs að kirkju þar,
hver einn var af hjarta fús
að hlusta á raddirnar.

Lýsti um húsið ljóminn sá,
leyndar raddir sungu,
undir með þá menjagná
mælti snjallri tungu:
„Þökk sé drottinn þér.
Besta skart og búninginn,
blessaður, gafstu mér.
Verði ætíð viljinn þinn
vor á meðal hér."

. . . . .

In ancient times there ruled in Rome
A certain king of the country.
He sentenced Christians to death,
Oppressed friends of the Lord,
Deprived them of life.

Diokletianus is
The wretch's name.
Innumerable saints
Lay in Helitisses.

The King appointed a man
To attend to this work.
Sinforianus is his name;
Books speak of it.
This one had a son.
One day, which is recorded,
He walked away from the table.
He then saw on the grounds
A beautiful woman.

Agnes was the name of the noble lady,
Fourteen years old,
Very fair and of shining virtue,
Chosen by the Lord
Ever to serve Him.
The bride was at prayers
Both day and night.
She made holy offerings,
Had little to do with the heathen.

Then the son of Sinforianus
Looks at the golden woman.
He liked the lady well.
He wanted to have the woman;
He offers a proposal.
She would not consider a heathen;
She was betrothed.
Then later she spoke to him:

"Remove yourself from me!"

With pained heart, in bitter misery
He walks home to the citadel;
Deathly ill of the mead of love.
It brought him sorrow
That he did not get the young woman.
He now told his father
Truthfully about this.
Sinforianus sent a man
To talk to the lady.

She said she had herself a lover,
So she did not want to marry.
"I am engaged to be married,
Therefore I could not
Incline to another, a worldly man."
"My bridegroom," spoke the maiden,
"Is the son of a virgin.
I shall, while my life lasts,
Love him with my heart.

"His bridal gift
Is goodness that never dwindles.
His reddish blood of roses
He daubs on my lips
Along with milk and honey.
Such delicacy satiates me
So that my heart is refreshed.
For love he let himself
Be wounded and nailed to a tree.

"He is also of the highest rank,
Over all worldly men.

It is impossible for you
To forbid his delight to me.
I trust implicitly
That nothing in the world
Can separate me from him.
I love him with all faithfulness
That will never diminish."

Then the messenger returns home
And reports everything.
Sinforianus replies to them,
"How strange it is
To see how stupid she is.
Who can it be in the circle of champions
That she intends for herself
Since I am of the highest rank in the land
And my son here?"

The pagan who had made the report
Replied first,
"There is no doubt
It is Jesus Christ
To whom she dedicates herself.
Mohammed has put forward
The men who rule here.
This heresy that I mention
Is a great harm, I feel."

The heathen women who served at the temple became startled.
With the girl they praised God
And the noise did not cease.
Then there was heard a loud noise.

The temple, full of wickedness,
Was turned into a church of God.
Everyone was eager in his heart
To listen to the voices.
A radiance glowed about the house,
Hidden voices sang.
Then the girl
Spoke with a brilliant tongue,
"Thanks, Lord, to You;
The best finery and raiment,
Blessed One, You gave to me.
May Your will always be among us here."

Mr. Valdimar Johnson
Riverton, Manitoba

137*

Utan lands í einum bý
ekkja fátæk byggði.
Fróm og guðhrædd geði í,
góðan lofstír fékk af því;
engan mann í athöfn sinni hún styggði.

Fleiri átti börn en brauð,
bar sig þó að gefa.
Sagði hún æ, í sinni nauð,
sig hafa nógu mikinn auð,
skyldi hún aldrei skaparans gæsku efa.

En svo bar til að hungrið hart
hennar þrengdi kosti.
Bjargarlaus með barnið margt
burtu gékk, því svo var vart.
Var þá úti vetrartíð með frosti.

Bak og fyrir börnin smá
bar hún langa vega,
hallæri þó herti á,
svo hvergi skyldi náttstað fá.
Mæddist hún af hungri og hörðum trega.

Bar hana einum brunni að,
björg þá litla kenndi
Settist niður á sama stað,
sér til hjálpar drottinn bað,
augunum sínum upp til himins renndi.

---

* See music transcription for this item on page 315.

Gullskorð ýmist grét eða bað,
gerði á raunir herða.
Voluðum börnum vatnið gaf,
vífið fyllti skikkjulaf;
að góðu sagði hún guð þeim léti það verða.

Litlu sídar sá hún mann
sá var fríður næsta.
Skrýddur hvítum skrúða hann,
skarlatsþöllu heilsa vann.
Vífið honum virðing veitti æðsta.

Maðurinn spyr: „Hvað þenkir þú
þínum nauðum hnekkir,
og hve lengi líf þitt nú?
Lítilfjörleg næring sú,
þú örmagnast þótt einsamalt vatnið drekkir."

„Einn er guð hinn sami sá,
sem seðja kann mig núna.
Þó engin kunni ég efni að sjá,
sem ekkjan í Sareftá:
á hann set ég alla mína trúna."

„Þú ert kona trúartraust,
trega þinn að stilla.
Gakk þú heim með geðið hraust,
því guð drottinn mun efalaust,
girnd þíns hjarta gera nú upp að fylla."

Síðan skildist hún við hann,
heim gékk aftur kæra.
Í því húsi olíu fann

svo út af hverju keri rann.
Lof sé guði, líka dýrð og æra.

Þeir sem seta son guds á
sína trú gervalla,
eflaust hefur ætíð sá
ólukkunni komist hjá,
þó megi honum kross og mótgangur tilfalla.

Dæmin kenna þessi þér
þolinmóður að vera,
því alla guð um síðir sér.
Samur í dag og gær hann er,
kappkostum því krossinn hans að bera.

. . . . .

In a foreign land, in a certain town
There lived a poor widow,
Pious and God-fearing in temperament.
She, therefore, had a good reputation;
She offended no man in his work.

She had more children than loaves of bread
But still gave some away.
In her need, she always said
That she had enough riches;
That she would never doubt the Creator's goodness.
But then it happened that severe hunger
Made her situation difficult.
Helpless, with many a child,
She walked away, such were the circumstances.
Outside there was then winter with frost.

Back and front the small children
She carried a long distance,
Even though the situation became so severe
That nowhere could she find a place to sleep.
She wearied of hunger and bitter sadness.

She came to a certain well,
Then realizing little help
Sat down in that same place,
Prayed to the Lord for help,
Directing her eyes toward heaven.

The woman either cried or prayed,
Her difficulties became greater.
She gave water to her miserable children.
The woman filled the fold of her cloak
And said God would let them derive good from it.

A little later she saw a man,
He was very handsome,
Wearing white vestments.
He greeted the woman.
The lady showed him utmost respect.

The man asks, "What do you think
Will stop your difficulties,
And how long your life now?
Slight is the nourishment,
You will collapse if you drink only water."

"That One is God, the same One,
Who can now satiate me.
Even though I may see no riches,

As the widow of Sareftá,
I put all my faith in Him."

"You are a woman of trusting faith
In your ability to calm your sadness.
Walk home hale in thought,
Because God the Lord will doubtless
Fulfill the desire of your heart."

Then she departed from him,
The beloved one walked back home.
In the house she found oil
So that each container overran.
Praise to God's glory and honour.

Those who place in God's Son
Their entire faith,
They will always, without doubt,
Escape ill fortune,
Even though suffering and resistance may befall
    them.

These examples teach you
To be patient,
Because eventually God attends to everyone.
He is the same today as yesterday;
Let us then strive to carry His cross.

Mrs. Sigþóra Tómasson
Hekla Island, Manitoba

138*

Á ég að láta það fara þó það sé ekki vel fallegt? Allt er einmitt-- einm. .-- einmitt eins og Guðrún heitin söng það. En hvort það er úr GRALLARANUM, eða hverju, já, það veit ég ekki.

> Spákona hét þar Anna ein
> af Asors barnaliði,
> Fanúelsdóttir, dygg og hrein,
> dýrkaði helga siði.

> Hafði sjö ár í hjarta klár
> hafði með engum manni
> meydómi frá, sem fræðin tjá,
> fannst oft í helgum ranni.

. . . . .

Should I let it go although it isn't very nice? It's all really-- real. .-- really like the late Guðrún sang it. But whether it is from the GRALLARANUM, or what, yes, that I don't know.

> A certain prophetess named Anna
> Of Asor's tribe,
> Daughter of Fanúel, virtuous and pure,
> Worshipped according to holy custom.

> For seven years, with pure heart,
> Had with no man
> Departed from virginity, according to writ;
> Was often found in a holy place.

Miss Anna Nordal
Gimli, Manitoba

---

* See music transcription for this item on page 315.

139*

Sjáđu, það er sagan af því, að það er mađur sem hafđi farid í einvígi og, auðvitað, hann særđist þar og hefur líklega verid búinn ađ drepa hinn, og-- nema hann s. . . . . . Það byrjar

> Þorgeir reið frá einvíginu og var sár.
> „Sækið þið hana Ingibjörgu áður en ég verð nár."
> Svona rætast sumra manna draumar.
>
> – „Ef þorir þú að signa þig með heilögum kross,
> ég skal faðma þig og kyssa hinn síðasta koss."
> Svona rætast sumra manna draumar.
>
> Í gröfina hinn dauði sté, en hárið svart
> Ingibjargar, næsta morgunn, var orðið silfurbjart.
> Svona rætast sumra manna draumar.

Hún varð ljós. .-- hvít á hærum á einni nótt, segir sagan.

. . . . .

See, it is the story of this man who had been in a duel and, of course, he was wounded, and had likely killed the other one, and-- except he s. . . . . . It begins:

> Þorgeir rode from the duel and was wounded.
> "Go and get Ingibjörg before I die."
> In this way are some men's dreams fulfilled.

---

* See music transcription for this item on page 316.

– "If you dare to bless yourself with a holy cross,
I will embrace you and kiss you the final kiss."
    In this way are some men's dreams fulfilled.

Into the grave the dead one stepped, but the black hair
Of Ingibjörg had become silver-bright the next morning.
    In this way are some men's dreams fulfilled.

She became light. .-- white-haired in one night, the story says.

Mr. Björn Bjarnason
Arborg, Manitoba

140

    Kátt er um jólin koma þau senn
    þá trúi ég að upp líti Gilsbakkamenn.
    Upp munu þeir líta og undra sig mest,
    úti sjá þeir stúlku á blesóttum hest.
    Úti sjá þeir stúlku sem umtalað var:
    „Þar sé ég að hér ríður Guðrún í garð,
    þar sé ég að hér ríður Guðrún mín heim."
    Út kom hann góði Þórður einn af þeim,
    út kom hann góði Þórður allra fyrst.
    Hann hefur fyrri Guðrúnu kysst,
    hann hefur fyrri gefið henni brauð,
    tekið hana af baki svo tapar hún nauð,
    tekið hana af baki og borið inn í bæ.
    „Komdu sæl og blessuð, keifaðu inn,
    kannske þú sjáir hann afa þinn.
    Kannske þú sjáir ömmu þar hjá,
    þínar fjórar systur og bræðurna þrjá,
    þínar fjórar systur sem fagna þér best.
    Af skal ég spretta og fóðra þinn hest,
    af skal ég spretta reiðtygin þín.
    Leiðið þér inn stúlkuna, Sigríður mín,
    leiðið þér inn stúlkuna og setið hana í sess."
    – „Já," segir Sigríður, „fús er ég til þess."
    „Já," segir Sigríður; kyssir hún fljóð.
    – „Má ég . . . sírópið, systir mín góð?"

Nei. Ég held ég sé nú . . . .

    „. . . veggina systir mín góð,
    rektu þig ekki á veggina, gaktu með mér."
    Koma þær að húsdyrum og sæmilega fer;

– "Má ég . . . sírópið, systir mín góð?"

Nei. Ég held ég sé nú . . . .

"... veggina systir mín góð,
rektu þig ekki á veggina, gaktu með mér."
Koma þær að húsdyrum og sæmilega fer;
koma þær að húsdyrum og tala ekki orð,
þar situr fólkið við tedrykkjuborð;
þar situr fólkið og drekkur svo glatt.
Innstur sat hann afi með parruk og hatt;
innstur sat hann afi og ansar um sinn:
"Komdu sæl og blessuð dóttir mín inn;
komdu sæl og blessuð sittu hjá mér.
Uppi er teið en bagalega fer,
uppi er teið en ráð er við því,
ég skal láta hita það aftur á ný;
ég skal láta hita það helst vegna þín.
Heilsaðu öllu fólkinu kindin mín,
heilsaðu öllu fólkinu og gerðu það nú rétt."
Kyssir hún á hönd sína og talar án móðs,
svo allir í húsinu óska henni góðs.
Svo allir í húsinu þegar í stað
taka til að gleðja hana og ganga þær inn
Guðný og Rósa með teketilinn,
Guðný og Rósa með glóðarker.
Þá ansaði hann afi, "það líkar mér,"
þá ansar hann afi á eldra Jón þá:
"Taktu ofan bollana og skenktu þar á;
taktu ofan bollana og gá þú að því,
sparaðu ekki sykurinn að hnippa þar í;
sparaðu ekki sykurinn því nóg hef ég til.

Allt vil ég gera Guðrúnu í vil;
allt vil ég gera fyrir það fljóð.
Má ég bjóða þér sírópið dóttir mín góð?
Má ég bjóða þér sírópið?" afi kvað.
– „Æ jú. Dáyndi þykir mér það,
æ jú. Dáyndi þykir mér te."
– „Má ég bjóða þér mjólkina, meira en svo sé?
Má ég bjóða þér mjólkina? Vilborg, fyrst,
vertu ekki lengi því stúlkan er þyrst;
vertu ekki lengi því nú liggur á."
Jón fer að skenkja bollana á;
Jón fer að skenkja og ekki er það spé:
Sírópið, mjólkina, sykur og te,
sírópið, mjólkina sýpur hún af list
þar til að ketillinn allt hefur misst,
þar til að ketillinn þurr er í grunn.
Þakkar hún fyrir með hönd og munn;
þakkar hún fyrir og þykist nú hress.
„Sittu nokkuð lengur til samlætis,
sittu nokkuð lengur, sú er mín bón."
Ansar hann afi á yngra Jón;
ansar hann afi, „komdu til mín,
sæktu ofan í kjallara messuvín;
sæktu ofan í kjallara messuvín og mjöð,
ég ætla að veita henni svo hún verði glöð,
ég ætla að veita henni vel um stund."
Jón kemur bráðum á föður síns fund,
Jón kemur bráðum með brennivínsglas.
Þrífur hann staupið, þó það sé mas;
þrífur hann staupið og steypir þar á.
Til er henni drukkið svo teigar hún á;
til er henni drukkið ýmislegt öl.

Glösin og skálarnar skerða henni böl;
glösin og skálarnar ganga þar í kring.
Gaman er að koma á svoddan þing,
gaman er að koma þá Guðný ber
ljósið í húsið og húma fer.
Ljósið í húsinu logar svo glatt,
amma gefur brauðið og er það nú satt;
amma gefur brauðið og ostinn með.
Margrét fer að skemmta með söngvara sið;
Margrét fer að skemmta og er henni sýnt.
Þá kemur Markús og dansar svo fínt;
þá kemur Markús í máldrykkjulok,
leikur hann fyrir með latínu-sprok;
leikur hann fyrir með listaþel.
Ljóðið er þrotið og lifi þér vel.

. . . . .

There is gaiety at yuletide, they will come soon,
Then I believe the men of Gilsbakki will look up,
They will look up and be most astonished.
Outside they see a girl on a blaze-marked horse;
Outside they see the girl being spoken of.
"There I see Guðrún riding into the yard,
There I see my Guðrún riding home."
Out came dear Þórður, one of them,
Out came dear Þórður, the very first,
He has kissed Guðrún before.
He has given her bread before,
Helped her off her mount to relieve her discomfort,
Helped her off her mount and carried her inside.
"Be happy and blessed!" he keeps saying,

"Be happy and blessed. Do amble in.
Perhaps you will see your grandfather,
Perhaps you will see your grandmother close by,
Your four sisters and three brothers,
Your four sisters who greet you most warmly.
I will unsaddle and feed your horse,
I will undo your riding gear.
Take the girl inside, Sigríður, my dear,
Take the girl inside and give her a seat."
– "Yes," says Sigríður, "gladly I'll do that."
"Yes," says Sigríður; kisses the lady.
– "May I . . . the syrup, my dear sister?"

No. I think I have . . . .

" . . . walls my good sister,
Don't bump into the walls, walk along with me."
They come to the house-door and all goes well;
They come to the house-door and do not speak a word.
There sit the people at a tea table,
There sit the people and drink so merrily.
Farthest in sits Grandfather with a peruke and hat,
Farthest in sits Grandfather and responds right away:
"Come in, be happy and blessed, my good daughter,
Come happy and blessed, sit by me.
The tea is finished, that's too bad,
The tea is finished, but there is a solution.
I will have it heated up again,
I will have it heated, especially for you.
Greet all the people, my pet,
Greet all the people and do it correctly."
She kisses her hand and was so elegant;

She kisses her hand and talks without tiring,
So all in the house wish her well.
So all in the house, right away,
Take to gladden her and that is the truth,
Take to gladden her, and in they walk,
Guđný and Rósa with the teakettle,
Guđný and Rósa with the chafing-dish.
Then Grandfather remarked, "That I like."
Then Grandfather remarks to Jón senior:
"Take the cups down and pour into them.
Take the cups down and make sure that
You don't spare the sugar to put into it,
Don't spare the sugar because I have plenty.
I want to do everything to please Guđrún,
I want to do everything to please that lady.
May I offer you the syrup my dear daughter?
May I offer you the syrup?" Grandfather says
– "Oh yes. I find it a delight,
Oh yes. I find tea a delight."
– "May I offer you the milk? More than that?"
– "May I offer you the milk? Vilborg, first,
Don't be long because the girl is thirsty,
Don't be long because we're in a hurry."
Jón starts to pour into the cups,
Jón starts to pour and that is no joke:
The syrup, the milk, sugar and tea.
The syrup, the milk she sips artfully,
Until the kettle is deprived of everything,
Until the kettle is completely dry.
She thanks him with hand and mouth,
She thanks him and feels refreshed.

"Sit a little longer, for company,
Sit a little longer, that is my request."
Grandfather remarks to the younger Jón,
Grandfather remarks, "Come here,
Fetch communion wine down from the cellar.
Fetch communion wine down from the cellar.
I'm going to serve her some to bring her cheer;
I'm going to give her plenty for a while."
Jón returns soon to his father;
Jón comes soon with a brandy glass.
He grabs the glass in spite of the commotion;
He grabs the glass and pours into it.
She is toasted, then she drinks;
She is toasted in all sorts of wine.
The drinks and the toasts diminish her discontent;
The drinks and the toasts make the round.
What fun it is to come to such a gathering;
What fun it is to come when Guđný carries
The light into the house at approaching dusk;
The light in the house burns so gaily.
Grandmother serves the bread and that is the truth;
Grandmother serves the bread along with the cheese.
Margrét begins to entertain in the manner of singers,
Margrét begins to entertain, and at that she is good.
Then Markús comes and dances so elegantly;
Then Markús comes at the end of the drink,
Entertains them with a Latin speech,
Entertains them with artful disposition.
The verses have come to an end, and now live well.

Mrs. Guđrún Pálsson
Arborg, Manitoba

MOCK NARRATIVES

141

Köttur úti í mýri
setti upp á sér stýri,
úti er ævintýri.

Þá enti maður á þessu, þegar maður var búin að þylja fyrir börnin lengi, búin að verða leið á því.

. . . . .

A cat in the marsh
Set up his rudder.
The story is finished.

One, then, ended on this when one had been reciting for the children for a long period, gotten tired of it.

Mrs. Hrund Skúlason
Winnipeg, Manitoba

142

Karl og kerling í koti sínu
áttu sér einn kálf,
og þá er sagan hálf.
Hann hljóp út um allan völl
og þá varð sagan öll.

Já.

. . . . .

A churl and a crone in their cot
Owned one calf,
And then the story is half told.
It ran all over the field
And then the story is all told.

Yes.

Mrs. Hrund Skúlason
Winnipeg, Manitoba

PROVERBS AND SAYINGS

143

Aldrei skyldi seinn maður flýta sér.

·····

A slow man should never go fast.

144

Á skammri stundu skiftast veður í lofti.

·····

The weather can change in a short time.

145

Allt er hey í harðindum.

·····

Everything is hay in hard times.

146

Ástarhugir ávallt saman rata.

·····

People in love somehow always find each other.

147

Á heimahaug er haninn frakkastur.

. . . . .

The rooster is bravest on his own dunghill.

148

Allur er varinn góður.

. . . . .

All caution is good.

149

Allt er betra en gatið þó illa sé bætt.

. . . . .

Anything is better than a hole even if it's badly mended.

150

Af litlu skal manninn marka.

. . . . .

A man will be known by little things.

151

Aldrei augu leyna ef ann kona manni.

. . . . .

A woman's eyes can never conceal her love for a man.

152

Af ávöxtunum skuluð þér þekkja þá.

. . . . .

You will know them by the fruit of their labour.

153

Augað er spegill sálarinnar.

. . . . .

The eye is the mirror of the soul.

154

Allir hafa eitthvað til síns ágætis.

. . . . .

Everything has something to recommend them.

155

Auðginnt er æskan.

. . . . .

Youth is easily enticed.

156

Allt er þegar þrennt er.

. . . . .

Three marks completion.

157

Allan skrattan vígja þeir.

. . . . .

All kinds of Devil's riffraff gets ordained.

158

Allt hold er hey.

. . . . .

All flesh is hay.

Proverbs and Sayings

159

Af misjöfnu þrífast börnin best.

. . . . .

Children thrive best on uneven variety.

160

Alltaf bætist raun á raun.

. . . . .

Trouble always follows trouble.

161

Allir hafa börnin verið.

. . . . .

Everyone has been a child.

162

Aldrei er góð vísa of oft kveðin.

. . . . .

Never is a good verse sung too often.

163

Allar gjafir girnast laun.

. . . . .

All gifts desire payment.

164

Allt er gott þá endirinn er góður.

. . . . .

Everything is good when the outcome is good.

165

Ástin er sterkari en hel.

(Ég get nú ekki útlistað þetta. Mér þykir nú þetta, þó ég skrifaði það niður, ekki góður málsháttur. [. . . .] Þessir málshættir eru barasta-- barasta tíndir upp af handahófi. Maður hefur lært þetta og gleymir því ekki.)

. . . . .

Love is stronger than death.

(I can't really explain this. I don't find this, although I wrote it down, a good proverb. [. . . .] These proverbs are just-- just picked up here and there. One has learned this and doesn't forget it.)

166

Betra seint en aldrei.

. . . . .

Better late than never.

167

Betra er autt rúm en illa skipað.

. . . . .

Better an empty berth than one which is badly appointed.

168

Bágur er hver búskapur, böl er hjúskapur, illt er einlífið, og að öllu er nokkuð.

. . . . .

Householding is difficult, marriage is a misery, the single life is bad, and something is wrong with all of them.

169

Betri er krókur en kelda.

. . . . .

A detour is better than a bog.

170

Betri er belgur en barn.

. . . . .

A bag [of food?] is better than a baby.

171

Blindur er bóklaus maður.

. . . . .

A man without a book is blind.

172

Betra er að veifa röngu tré en öngu.

. . . . .

It is better to swing the wrong stick than none at all.

Proverbs and Sayings

173

Brennt barn forðast eldinn.

. . . . .

A burnt child avoids the fire.

174

Brjóta skal bein til mergjar.

. . . . .

A bone should be broken to its marrow.

175

Betur má ef duga skal.

. . . . .

Better do it well if it is to last.

176

Best er illu aflokið.

. . . . .

Best to be done with the unpleasant task.

177

Ber er hver að baki sér nema bróður eigi.

Gunnlaugur Holm: Þetta sagði Grettir.
Fríða Holm: Þetta sagði nú Grettir Ásmundsson.

. . . . .

Exposed is a man's back unless he has a brother.

G.H.: Grettir said that.
F.H.: Grettir Ásmundsson said that.

178

Bústu við því illa því það góða skaðar þig eigi.

. . . . .

Expect the bad because the good won't hurt you.

179

Barnslán er betra en fé.

. . . . .

Luck with children is better than wealth.

180

Böl er barn í draumi nema sveinbarn-- barn sé og sjálfur eigi.

(Þetta mun vera eftir-- eftir álfkonu.)

· · · · ·

A child in a dream foretells hardship unless it's a male child-- child and is one's own.

(This is reputed to be from-- from a fairy woman.)

181

Betri er fullur magi en fagur kyrtill.

· · · · ·

A full stomach is better than a fair tunic.

182

Betri er heilt en vel gróið.

· · · · ·

Whole is better than well healed.

183

Betra er hjá sjálfum sér að taka en bróður að biðja.

. . . . .

Better to take from oneself than to ask a brother.

184

Bundinn er sá örn sem skætir.

. . . . .

The eagle that taunts is encumbered.

185

Bragð er að, þá barnið finnur.

. . . . .

There is flavour when a child tastes it.

186

Deila djarfráðir þótt dauðir séu báðir.

. . . . .

The rash keep debating even after they're dead.

187

Dag skal að kvöldi lofa.

. . . . .

At eve, praise the day.

188

Dyggð er gulli dýrmætari.

. . . . .

Virtue is more precious than gold.

189

Dauðinn er þeim kær sem hamingjan er mótbær.

. . . . .

Death is dear to those to whom fortune is opposed.

190

Dramb er falli næst.

. . . . .

Arrogance is nearest to a fall.

191

Drjúg eru morgunverkin.

. . . . .

Morning labours go far.

192

Dýrt er drottins orðið.

. . . . .

The word of the Lord is precious.

193

Enginn er annars bróðir í leik.

. . . . .

No one is another's brother at games.

194

Einsdæmin eru verst.

. . . . .

Exceptional instances are the worst.

195

Enginn verður góður af engu.

. . . . .

No one becomes good from nothing.

196

Ellin er ljúf hinum vísu.

. . . . .

Old age is gentle to the wise.

197

Ekki margt, en þó mikið.

. . . . .

Not many, but much, nevertheless.

198

Enginn vægir varginum, og engu vægir vargurinn.

. . . . .

No one spares the beast of prey, and the beast of prey spares no one.

199

Ég sver það sem Helgi sver.

(Það er í sögu sjálfsagt. Það er vafalaust í sögu. Já.)

. . . . .

I swear to what Helgi swears to.

(It's probably in a story. It is doubtlessly in a story. Yes.)

200

Ekki liggur á; enginn segir: "Flýttu þér."

. . . . .

There is no urgency; no one says, "Hurry up."

201

Engin ósköp standa lengi.

. . . . .

No upheaval lasts for long.

202

Enginn ræður sínum næturstað.

. . . . .

No one can will their night's abode.

203

Ekki veldur sá varir, þó verr fari.

·····

The one who cautions isn't responsible if things go worse than anticipated.

204

Eins dauði er annars líf.

·····

One man's death is another's life.

205

Ekki er allt gull sem glóir.

·····

Not all that glitters is gold.

206

Ekki sér á svörtu.

(Þetta er nú ekki réttur málsháttur.)

·····

Black hides dirt.

(This proverb is not correct.)

207

Ekkert er ofgert fyrir vini sína.

. . . . .

Nothing is too much for one's friends.

208

Ég hafði hlaup en ekkert kaup.

. . . . .

I got some running around but no pay.

209

Ekki er gaman á ferðum.

. . . . .

There is no fun on journeys.

210

Eins og þú heilsar öðrum, heilsa ég þér.

. . . . .

As you greet others, I will greet you.

Proverbs and Sayings

211

Ég brenni mig ekki aftur á sama soðinu.

. . . . .

I won't burn myself again on the same broth.

212

Enginn veit sína ævina fyrr en öll er.

(Sumir vita það.)

. . . . .

No one knows their life until it's at an end.

(Some know it.)

213

Enginn er verri þó hann vakni.

. . . . .

No one is worse for waking up.

214

Er það nú vit í vettlings fit!

. . . . .

What wisdom in the crease of a mitten!

215

Enginn kemur öðrum meiri.

. . . . .

No one arrives greater than another.

216

[Laughter.] Enginn veit hvað au. .-- aur. .-- hvers aurvana nýtur þá andinn þrýtur. [Laughter.]

. . . . .

[Laughter.] No knows what the pe. .-- pen. .-- what the penniless enjoys when the spirit departs. [Laughter.]

217

Fullir kunna flest ráð.

. . . . .

The inebriated have all the answers.

218

Fyrr má nú rota en dauðrota.

· · · · ·

You can knock someone out without knocking them dead.

219

Farðu hægt svo þú komist áfram.

· · · · ·

Go slowly if you want to move forward.

220

Fjarlægðin gerir fjöllin blá og mennina mikla.

· · · · ·

Distance makes the mountains blue and men great.

221

Fáir kunna sig í góðu veðri heiman að búa.

· · · · ·

Few know how to prepare themselves when leaving home in good weather.

222

Fyrr er fullt en útaf flóir.

. . . . .

Full comes before flowing over.

223

Flas er sjaldan til fagnaðar.

. . . . .

Rashness seldom makes for happiness.

224

Fár veit hverju fagna skal.

. . . . .

Few know what to welcome.

225

Fé er jafnan fóstri líkt.

. . . . .

Animals invariably behave as they were raised.

Proverbs and Sayings

226

Fátt er svo með öllu illt að ekki boði nokkuð gott.

. . . . .

Few things are so evil that they don't point to some good.

227

Góður er hver genginn, illur aftur fenginn.

. . . . .

Whoever has moved on is good, bad if he returns.

228

Góð ráð eru peningsvirði.

. . . . .

Good advice is worth money.

229

Geđprýđi er gulli dýrri.

(Pađ er satt.)

. . . . .

A pleasant temperament is more precious than gold.

(That's true.)

230

Hverjum þykir sinn fugl fagur, þó hann sé bæđi ljótur og magur.

. . . . .

Everyone thinks his own bird is beautiful although he is both ugly and meagre.

231

Heggur sá er hlífa skyldi.

. . . . .

The one who's attacking should be shielding.

232

Hvað skal hundur til hofs eða köttur til kirkju?

. . . . .

What business does a dog have in a temple or a cat in a kirk?

233

Hver vill sínum fugli á flot koma.

. . . . .

Each one wants to set his own bird afloat.

234

Hátt hreykir heimskan sér.

. . . . .

Stupidity struts itself prominently.

235

Hallur er heimafenginn baggi.

. . . . .

The pack carried from home tends to totter.

236

Hætt er einu auganu nema vel fari.

. . . . .

One eye is in danger unless things go well.

237

Hamingjunni sé lof og dýrð, og Þórði mínum þakkir.

(Þetta hefur nú verið gömul kona, sjáðu.)

. . . . .

Praise and glory to Good Fortune, and thanks to my Þórður.

(This must have been an old woman, see.)

238

Hált er heims glysið.

. . . . .

Slippery is the world's frippery.

Proverbs and Sayings

239

Heimskum er best heima að sitja.

· · · · ·

The stupid should sit at home.

240

Hún hló með honum öllum.

· · · · ·

She laughed with the whole of it.

241

Hold er mold hverju sem það klæðist.

· · · · ·

Flesh is earth no matter how it's clothed.

242

Hátíð er til heilla best.

· · · · ·

A festive time is best for omens.

243

Hjúin gera garðinn frægan.

. . . . .

The servants give the household renown.

244

Að hika er sama og tapa.

. . . . .

To hesitate is the same as to lose.

245

Hver er sjálfum sér næstur.

. . . . .

Each is closest to his own self.

246

Hljóður er barnlaus bær.

. . . . .

Quiet is a childless house.

247

Hvað höfðingjarnir hafast að, hinir ætla sér leyfistað.

. . . . .

What aristocrats do, others take as license to emulate.

248

Heimskur er jafnan höfuðstór.

. . . . .

A stupid person invariably has a big head.

249

Það er þykkt blóð sem ekki rennur til skyldunnar.

. . . . .

Thick is the blood that doesn't run toward kinfolk.

250

Illt er illur að vera.

. . . . .

It's hard being wicked.

251

Illur á sér ills von.

.....

The wicked person expects wickedness.

252

Illt er að ken. .-- ke. .-- að kenna gömlum hundi að sitja.

.....

It's hard to tea. .-- te. .-- to teach an old dog to sit.

253

Í raun skal mann reyna.

.....

Through trials a man will be tested.

254

Kemst þó hægt fari.

.....

He gets there, however slowly.

255

Laglega fara lítið má.

. . . . .

Small can look nice.

256

Lítið hugsast litlu fólki.

. . . . .

Little occurs to little people.

257

Lengi tognar hrátt skinn.

. . . . .

Raw hide stretches far.

258

Lítið er ungs manns gaman.

. . . . .

It takes little to entertain a young man.

259

Mikið má ef vel vill.

. . . . .

Much can be accomplished if there is good will.

260

Mjór er mikils vísir.

. . . . .

The thin are wise about many things.

261

Mikill-- mikið vill meira.

. . . . .

Great-- much wants more.

262

Með litlu skal lítið drýgja.

. . . . .

Little can be eked out with little.

263

Maður veit hverju maður sleppir, en ekki hvað maður hreppir.

. . . . .

One knows what one lets go, but not what one will get.

264

Margir ágirnast meira en þarf.

. . . . .

Many lust for more than they need.

265

Mín er æran, víða lítillætið.

. . . . .

Mine is the honour, the humility widespread.

266

Margt er sér til gamans gert.

. . . . .

Many are the things one does for amusement.

267

Margt verður skáldunum að orði.

. . . . .

Many are the things that poets put into words.

268

Margur verður sá vís sem árla rís.

. . . . .

Many become wise who rise early.

269

Með lögum skal land byggja.

. . . . .

With laws the land shall be built.

270

Meira vinnur vit en strit.

. . . . .

Intelligence accomplishes more than toil.

271

Meðalhófið er best.

·····

Moderation is best.

272

Með illu skal illt út reka.

·····

Evil shall be driven out with evil.

273

Nota flest í nauðum skal, því nú er ekki betra val.

·····

Most things can be used in a pinch, because now there is no better choice.

274

Oft er flagð undir fögru skinni.

·····

One often finds a witch under fair skin.

275

Oft veltir lítil þúfa þungu hlassi.

. . . . .

A small bump often upsets a big load.

276

Sjón er sögu ríkari.

. . . . .

Seeing is better than hearing the story.

277

Sannleikann verður hver sá reiðastur.

. . . . .

The truth angers most.

278

Sjaldan liggur köttur í feigs manns fleti.

. . . . .

A cat seldom lies in the bed of one who is fey.

279

Ristu velgerðir á marmara, en mótgerðir á sand.

·····

Etch kindnesses in marble, but injuries in sand.

280

Sínum augum lítur hver á silfrið.

·····

Each looks at the silver with his own eyes.

281

Syngur hver fugl með sínu nefi.

·····

Each bird sings with his own beak.

282

Sæll er sá sem aldrei verst góðu.

·····

Happy is he who never fends off the good.

283

Sumir þykjast hafa sannleik allan sér í hendi.

. . . . .

Some think they have all truth in their hand.

284

Svo lengi lærir sem lifir.

. . . . .

You learn as long as you live.

285

Sveltur sitjandi krákum, fljúgandi fær.

(Svo er nú ekki meira af þessu hér.)

. . . . .

Sitting crows starve, flying ones catch.

(There isn't any more of this here.)

Mr. Gunnlaugur Holm
Vancouver, British Columbia

286

Ekki er allt gull sem glóir.

· · · · ·

Not all is gold that glitters.

287

Sjaldan er gott oflaunað nema með illu.

· · · · ·

Kindness is seldom too well repayed, unless it's with wickedness.

288

Oft er flagð undir fögru skinni, og dyggð undir dökkum hárum.

· · · · ·

Often there is a witch under fair skin, and virtue under dark hair.

289

Sjaldan er góð vísa of oft kveðin.

· · · · ·

Seldom is a good verse sung too often.

290

Sjaldan brýtur gæfumaður gler eða lukkumaður leir.

. . . . .

A fortunate man seldom breaks glass, or a lucky man pottery.

291

Sitt er hvað, gæfa eða gjörvileiki.

. . . . .

Good fortune and ability are two different things.

292

Sjaldan er ein báran stök.

. . . . .

You seldom have one wave by itself.

293

Ungur má en gamall skal.

. . . . .

The young may, but the old will.

Proverbs and Sayings

294

Ekki er allt með felldu.

. . . . .

Not everything fits as well as it should.

295

Oft sér betur auga en augu.

. . . . .

Eye often sees better than eyes.

296

Sá hlær best sem síðast hlær.

. . . . .

He laughs best who laughs last.

297

Margt er lítið ungs manns gaman.

. . . . .

Small are many of the entertainments of young men.

298

Margur heldur mig sig dyggan taka.

. . . . .

Many think that I see them as being virtuous.

299

Best er að taka gæsina þegar hún gefst.

. . . . .

It's best to drag the goose when it's available.

300

Ekki er vitið meira en guð gaf, því hrafninn tók það hálft af.

. . . . .

The intelligence isn't more than God gave, because the raven took half.

301

Frændur eru frændum verstir.

. . . . .

Kinsmen are worst to kinsmen.

302

Sá verður að vægja sem vitið hefur meira.

. . . . .

He who has the greater intelligence has to yield.

303

Illt er í ætt að girnast.

. . . . .

It's bad to lust for lineage.

304

Ekki er bagi þó bróðir sé nefndur.

. . . . .

It isn't a disadvantage to be called a brother.

305

Í þörfinni er þrællinn þekkur.

. . . . .

In time of need the thrall is appreciated.

306

Margur er knár þó hann sé lágur, og linur þó hann sé langur.

. . . . .

Many are strong although small, and limp although long.

307

Margt smátt gerir eitt stórt.

. . . . .

Many a little thing can make one large one.

308

Oft skellur hurð nærri hælum.

. . . . .

Often a door slams shut too close to the heel.

309

Oft kreppir skór að fæti.

. . . . .

A shoe often pinches the foot.

310

Sannleikurinn er sagna bestur, samt er hann ekki alltaf þægur gestur.

. . . . .

Truth makes for the best story, but it isn't always an easy guest.

311

Fátt segir af einum.

. . . . .

Few things are told of one man.

312

Margt er manna bölið, misjafnt drukkið ölið.

. . . . .

Many are the misfortunes of man; the ale is imbibed in dissimilar fashion.

313

Bágt er í tvö horn að líta.

. . . . .

It's difficult to keep an eye on two corners.

314

Sjón er sögu ríkari.

. . . . .

Seeing is better than hearing the story.

315

Margur hyggur auð í annars garði.

. . . . .

Many assume there is wealth in another's estate.

316

Oft verður lítið úr því högginu sem hátt er reitt.

. . . . .

Little often comes from the blow struck from high up.

317

Ekki eru það allt vinir sem hlæja.

. . . . .

Not all who laugh are friends.

318

Sjaldan kemur skúr úr heiðskíru lofti.

.....

Seldom is there a shower from a clear sky.

319

Ekki verður feigum forðað né ófeigum í hel komið.

.....

The fey can not be saved, and those who are not fey cannot be forced into the land of the dead.

320

Glöggt er gests augað.

.....

The guest's eye is perceptive.

321

Sætur er sjódauði, en vesæll vatnsdauði.

.....

A sea-death is sweet, but a fresh-water death is miserable.

322

Sulturinn gerir sætan mat.

. . . . .

Hunger makes food tasty.

Mr. Valdimar Johnson
Riverton, Manitoba

Proverbs and Sayings

323

Oft er flagð undir fögru skinni.

. . . . .

There is often a witch under fair skin.

324

Oft er vargslegur vormorgunn.

. . . . .

A spring morning often looks savage.

325

Morgunnroðinn vætir en kvöldroðinn bætir.

. . . . .

Red sky in the morning brings rain, but a red sky in the evening brings improvement.

326

Ekki er allt sem sýnist.

. . . . .

Not everything is as it seems.

327

Ekki er allt gull sem glóir.

. . . . .

Not everything is gold that glitters.

328

Margt smátt gerir eitt stórt.

. . . . .

Many small things make one large one.

329

Oft lætur hátt í tómri tunnu.

. . . . .

An empty barrel often makes a big noise.

330

Sá hlær best sem síðast hlær.

. . . . .

He laughs best who laughs last.

Mrs. Indiana Sigurðsson
Arborg, Manitoba

Proverbs and Sayings

331

Gefur guđ í gerđa spyrđu.

.....

God provides for the prepared [fish] stringer.

**Miss Anna Nordal
Gimli, Manitoba**

332

Ég kann ekki þessa lokalygi lengur.

.....

I don't know any more of this long lie.

**Mrs. Steinunn Valgarđsson
Gimli, Manitoba**

MUSIC TRANSCRIPTIONS

Carmelle Bégin, Ph. D.

Music Transcriptions

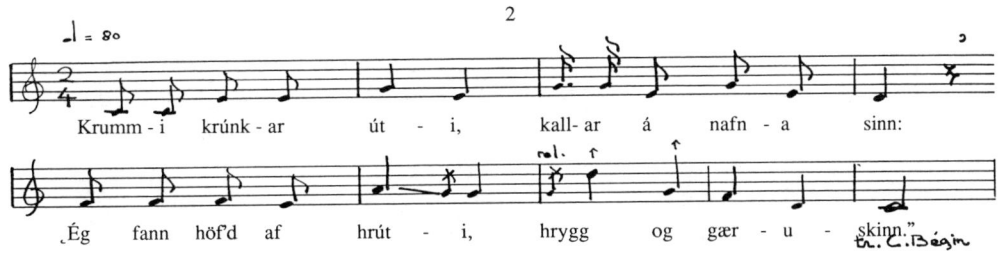

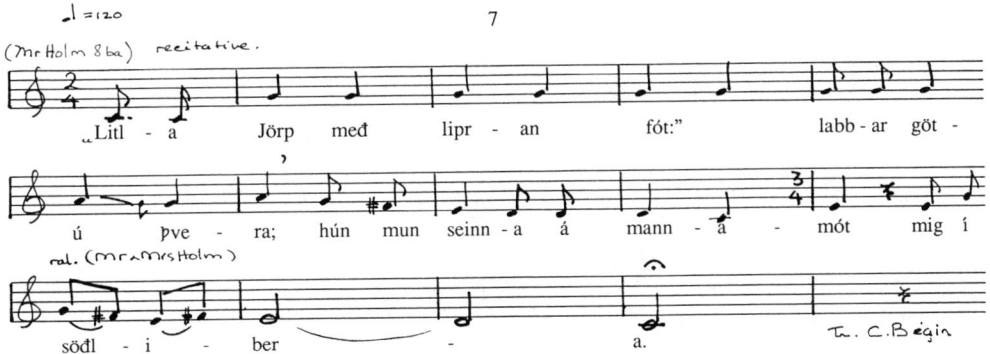

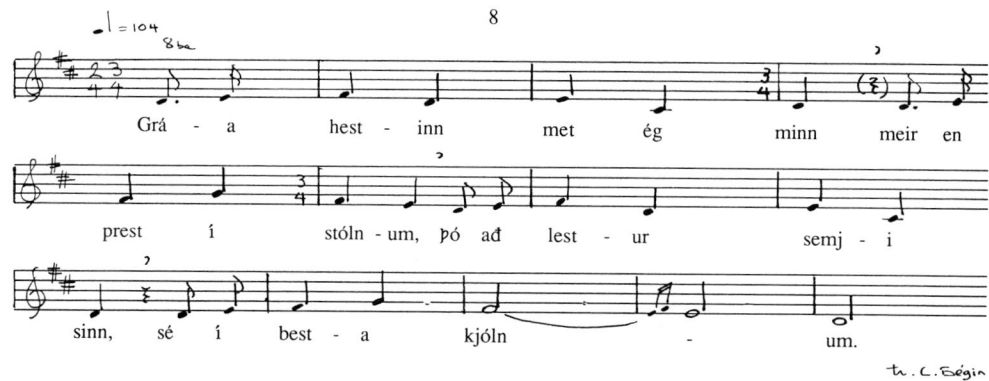
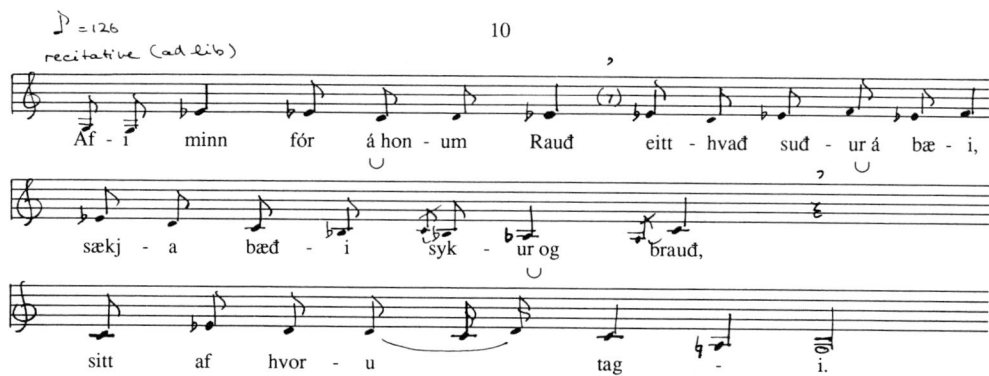

Music Transcriptions

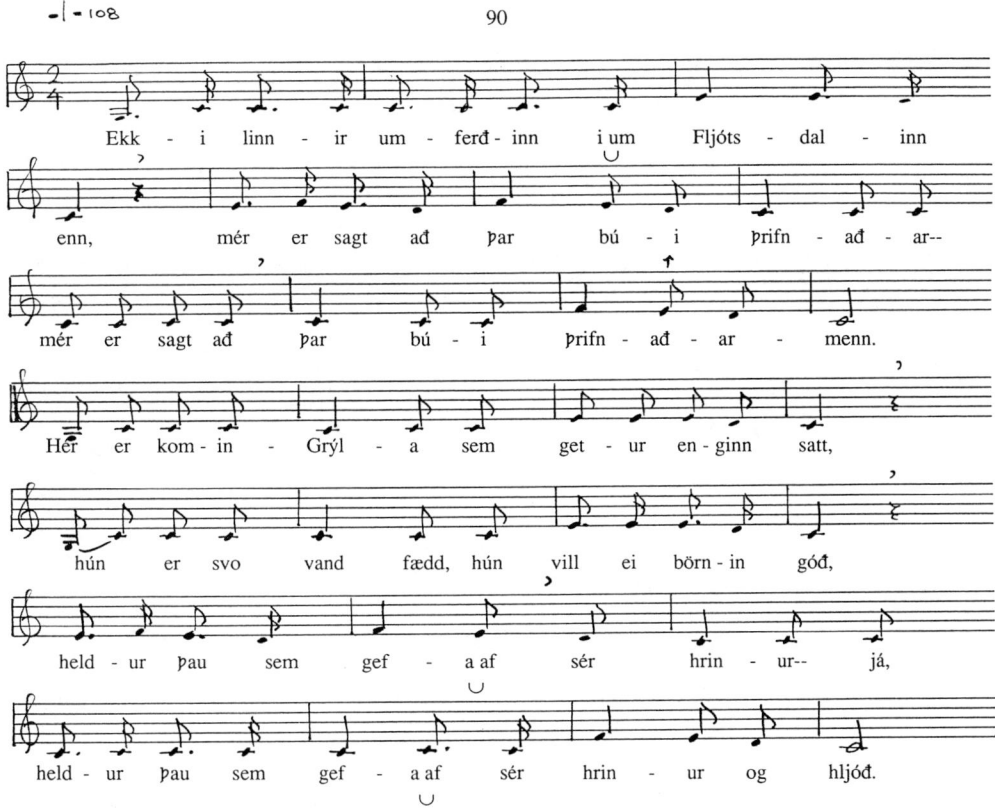

302   Icelandic-Canadian Memory Lore

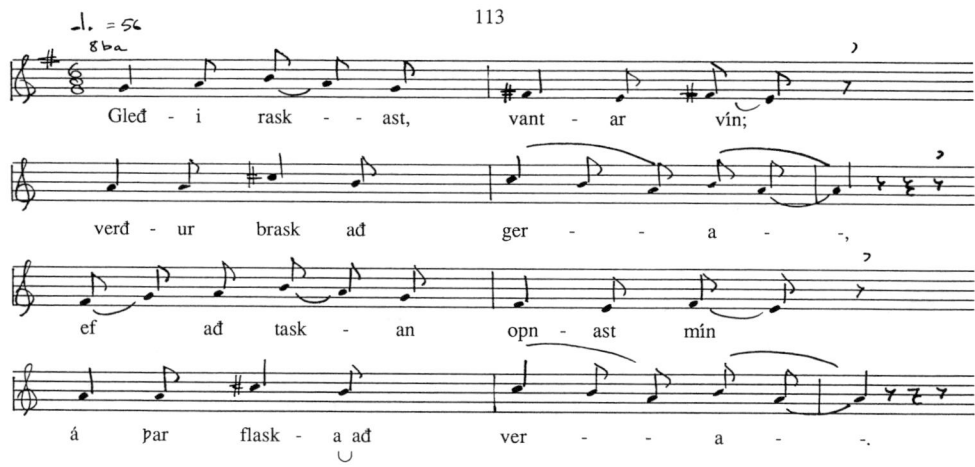

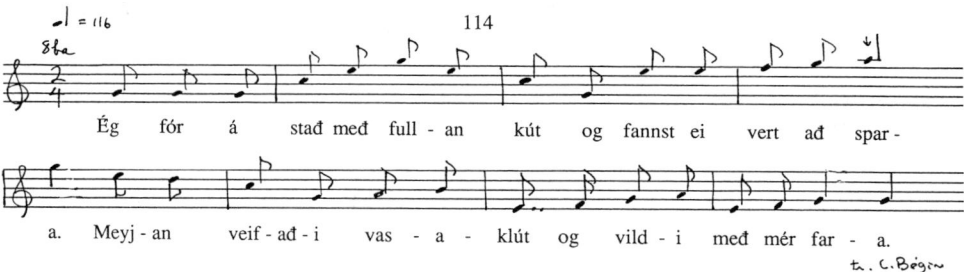

Music Transcriptions

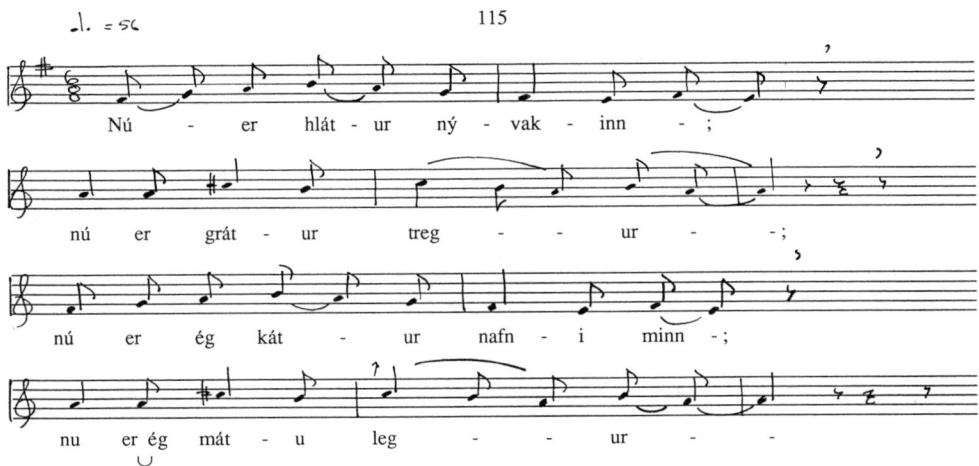

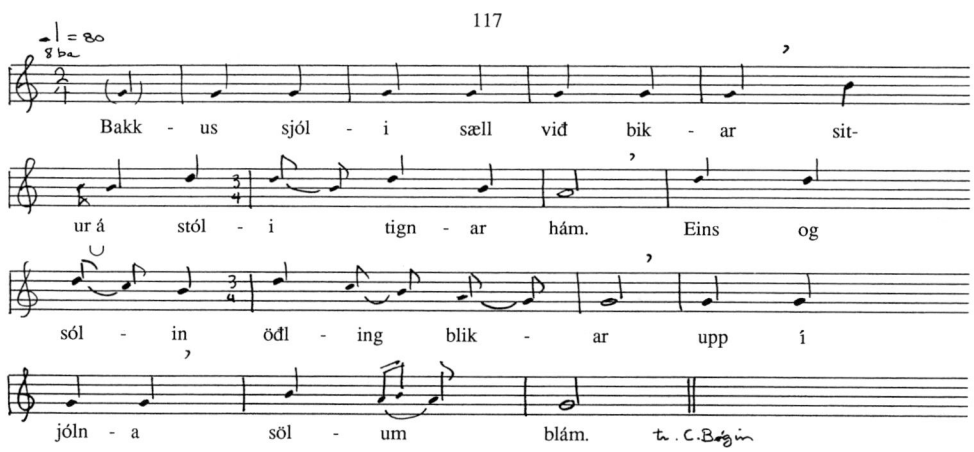

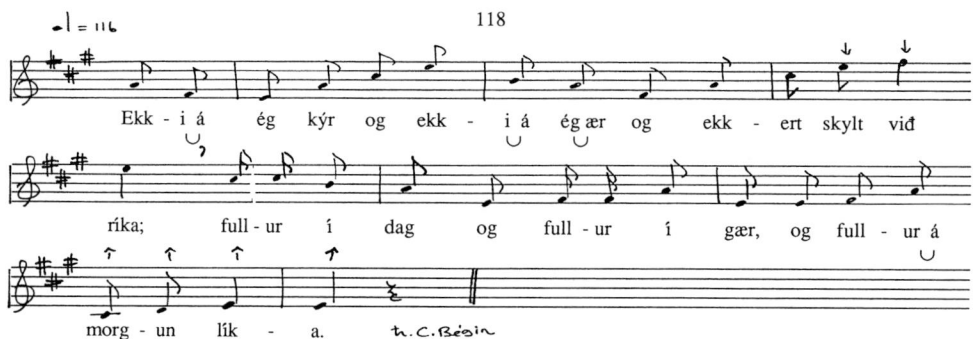

Music Transcriptions

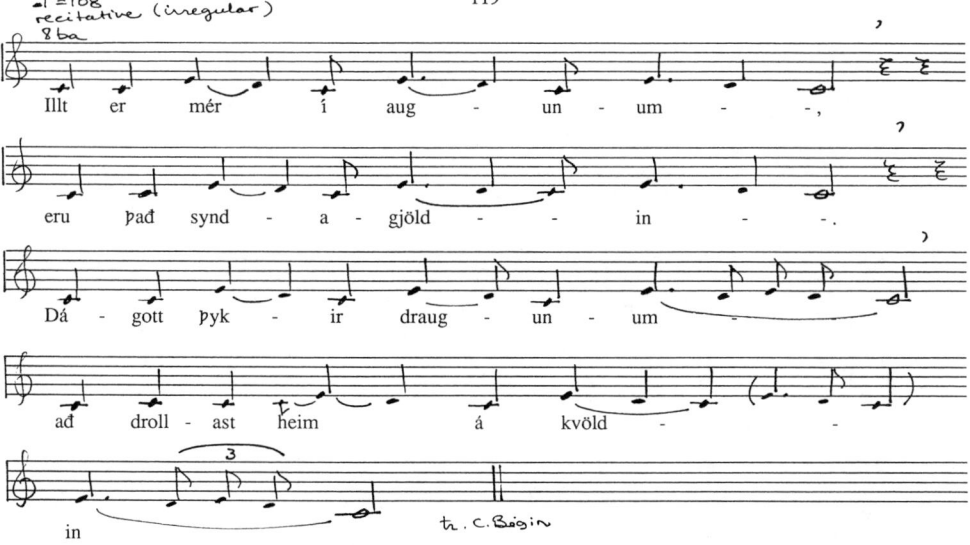

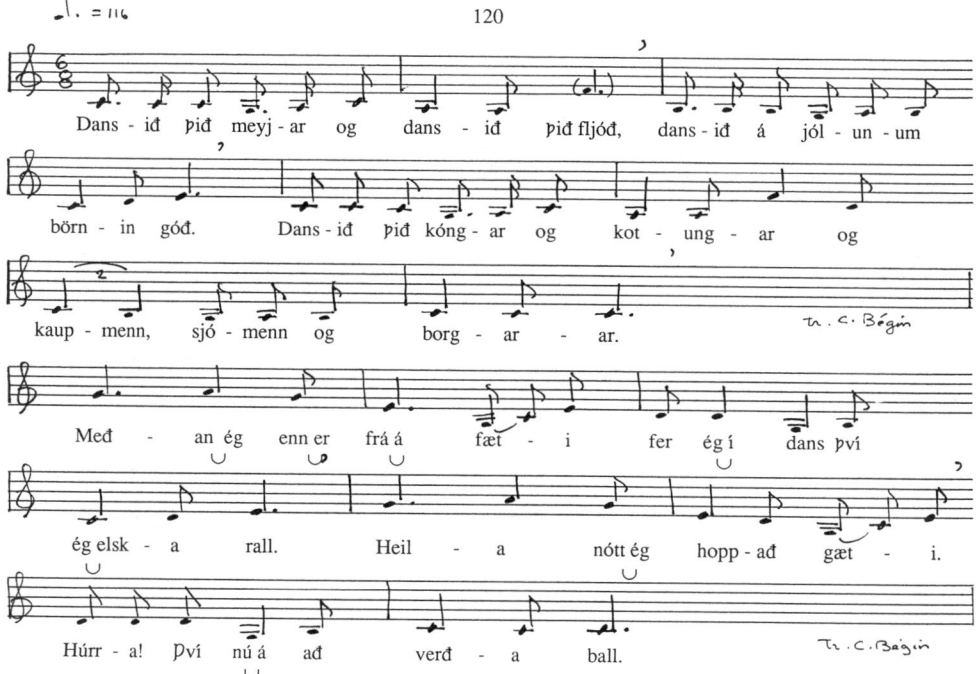

Music Transcriptions

307

Music Transcriptions

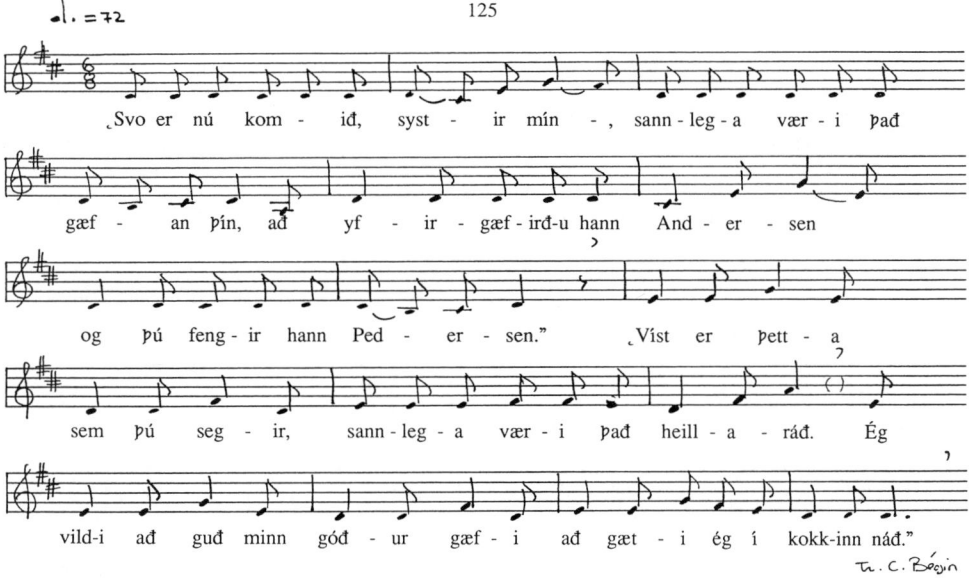

Music Transcriptions

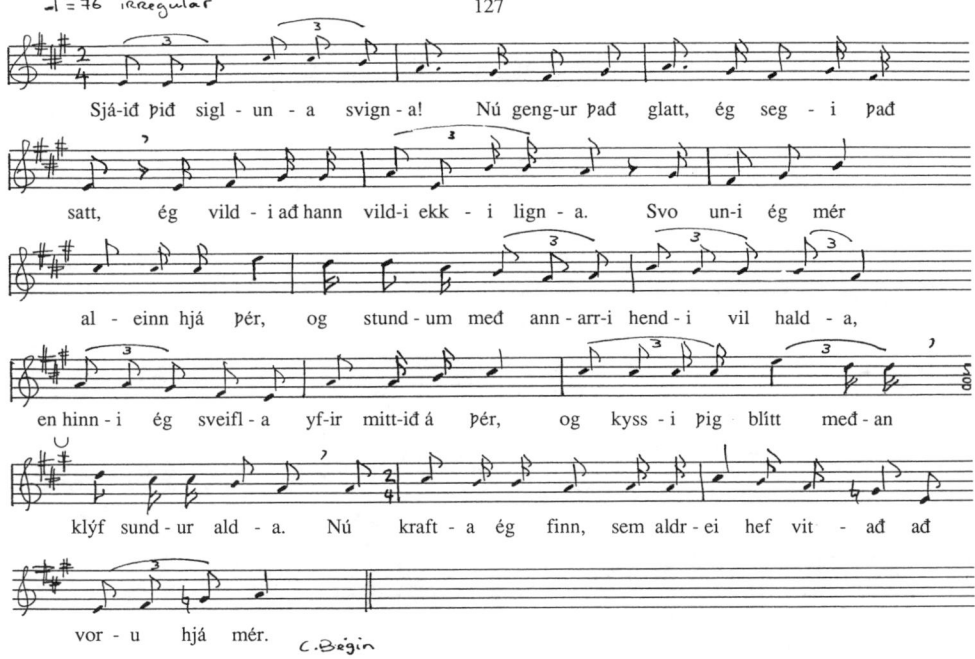

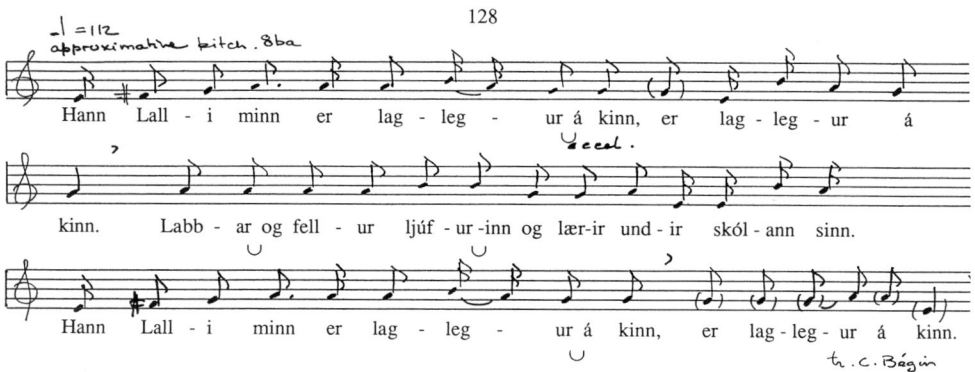
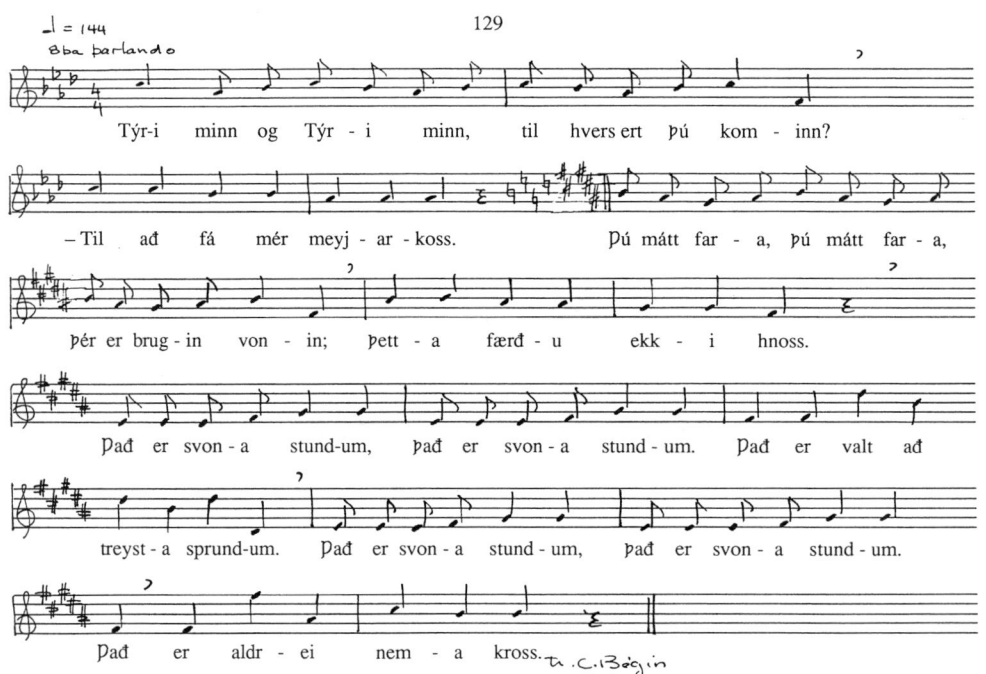

Music Transcriptions

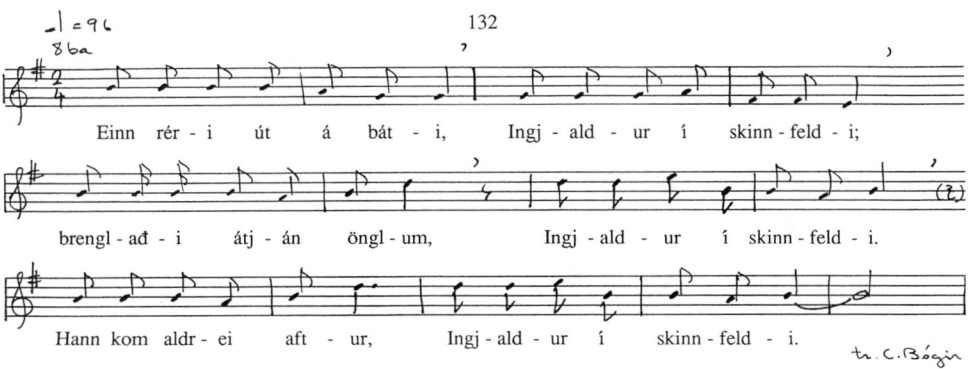

Icelandic-Canadian Memory Lore

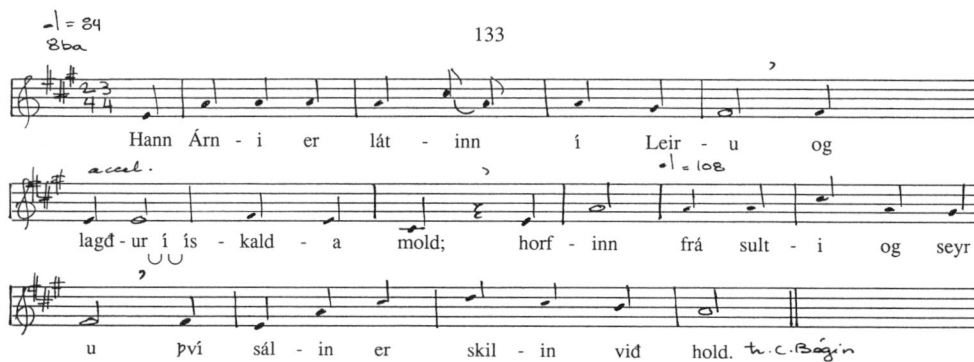

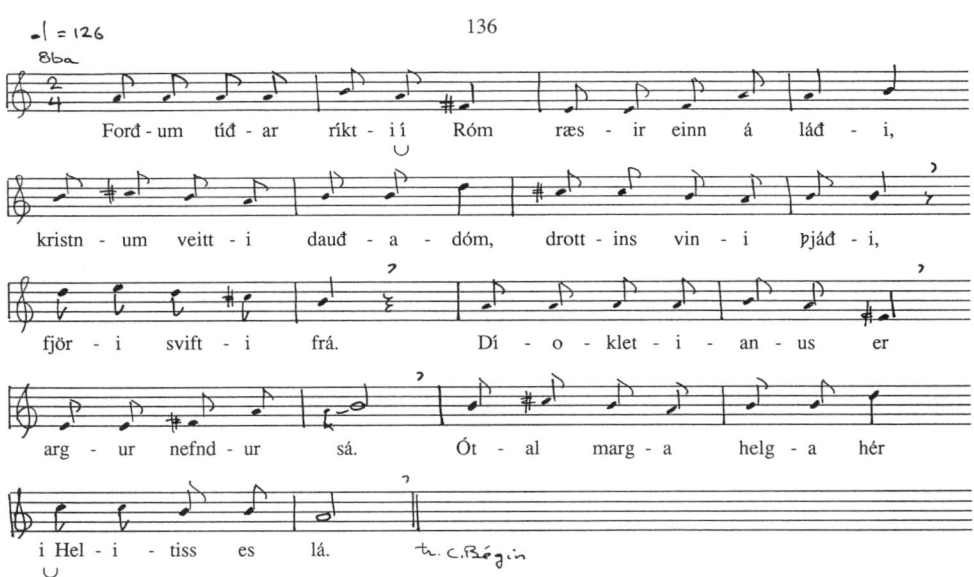

Music Transcriptions

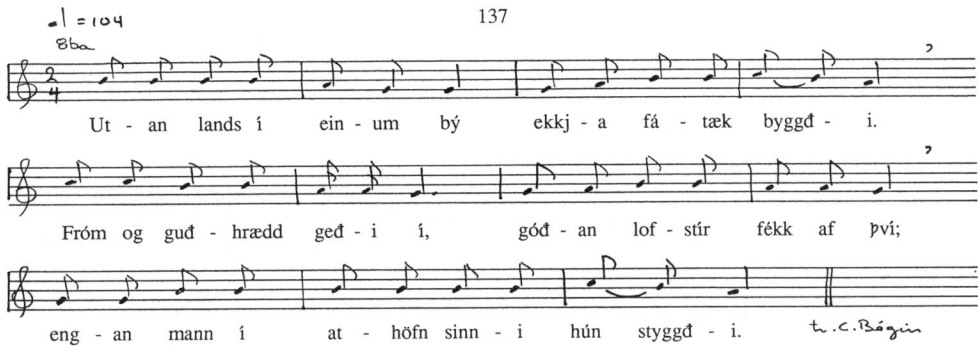

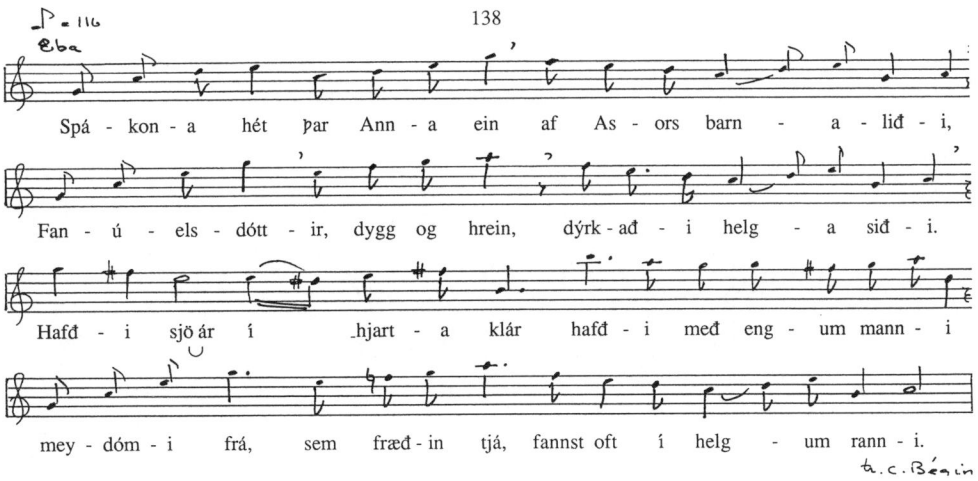

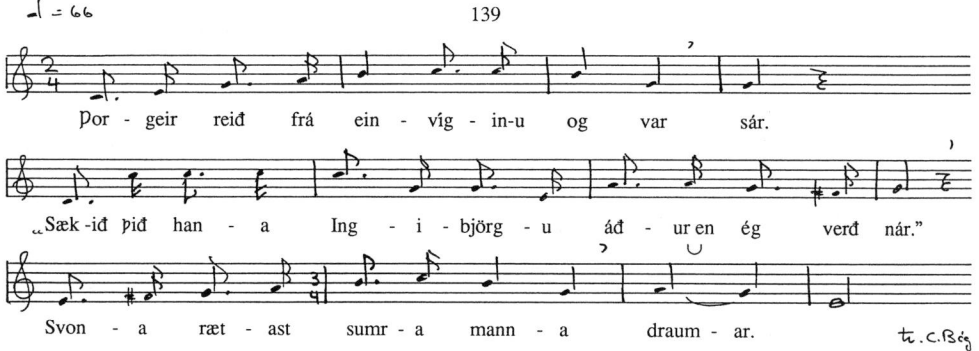

NOTES

NOTES

1) Recorded in Winnipeg, Manitoba, October 16, 1969 from Mrs. Hrund Adamsdóttir Skúlason; born in 1908 in Eyjafjörđur, northern Iceland; arrived in Canada in 1919; farmed with husband near Arborg, Manitoba, and later worked as a librarian at the University of Manitoba in Winnipeg.

The bird described in the poem, the <u>már</u>, is a type of sea gull.

For comparative published materials see: Ó.D.,* IV, 244; and S.S., XV, 27.

C.C.F.C.S. Einarsson Collection: MU-B-44. 2275.

2) Recorded in Vancouver, British Columbia, August 12, 1969 from Mrs. Svanfríđur (Fríđa) Jakobsdóttir Holm; born 1885 in Eyjafjörđur, northern Iceland; arrived in Canada in 1907; farmed with husband near Arborg, Manitoba, but after 1947 in Vancouver.

<u>Krummi</u> is the popular designation for a raven.

For comparative published materials see: S.S., XV, 27.

C.C.F.C.S. Einarsson Collection: MU-B-36. 1742. 3.

3) Recorded in Gimli, Manitoba, August 20, 1966 from Mrs. Sigríđur Pálsdóttir Björnsson; born 1885 in Ólafsfjörđur, northern Iceland; arrived in Canada in 1894; housewife in Arborg and Riverton, Manitoba, and in later life, for twenty years, in Winnipeg before retiring to Gimli.

The informant, blind at the time of this interview, says she is glad that she learned so many poems and rhymes as a child, because they help her to pass the time since she can no longer read.

C.C.F.C.S. Einarsson Collection: MU-B-1. 91.

4) Recorded from Mrs. Sigríđur Björnsson. See note no. 3, above.

C.C.F.C.S. Einarsson Collection: MU-B-1. 93.

---

* See key to abbreviations on P. 349.

5) Recorded in Blaine, Washington, August 7, 1969 from Mr. Sigurjón (Jón) Sigurðsson Mýrdal; born 1879 on Hecla Island, Lake Winnipeg, Manitoba; farmed at Point Roberts, Washington, and also worked as a carpenter and a mechanic for the local fishing industry.

C.C.F.C.S. Einarsson Collection: MU-B-34. 1588.

6) Received in a letter from Baldur, Manitoba, August 16, 1967, written by Mrs. Sigurveig Sveinsson; born 1890 in Argyle, Manitoba; she farmed with her husband near Baldur, Manitoba.

For comparative published materials see: Ó.J.Ó., 83.

C.C.F.C.S. Einarsson Collection: MU-C-6.1 (folio 11, item no. 1).

7) Recorded in Vancouver, British Columbia, August 12, 1969 from Mrs. Svanfríður Holm (see note no. 2, above) and, as primary informant, her husband, Mr. Gunnlaugur Haraldsson Holm; born 1884 in Eyjafjörður, northern Iceland; arrived in Canada in 1905; farmed near Arborg, Manitoba; after 1947 he worked mostly in Vancouver as a carpenter and a housepainter.

The reciting of his grandmother's verse triggered the informant's memory of the second, better-known, verse which he sang with his wife joining in on the last line.

C.C.F.C.S. Einarsson Collection: MU-B-36. 1742 .4 and .5. In the same collection are similar items recorded from Mr. Jón Pálsson (MU-B-8. 839), and from Mr. Gunnar Alexander (MU-B-22. 1108).

8) Recorded in Winnipeg, Manitoba, August 16, 1966 from Mr. Páll Hallgrímsson Hallson; born 1897 in Húnavatnssýsla, northern Iceland; arrived in Canada in 1913; grocer.

The informant sang this verse at interviewer's request. He identifies himself strongly as a Skagfirðingur (i.e. one whose ancestry is from Skagafjörður in northern Iceland), and, as such, regards himself as a light-hearted fellow, a lover of drink, horses and women.

C.C.F.C.S. Einarsson Collection: MU-B-1. 12.

9) Recorded in the Geysir district, near Arborg, Manitoba, August 29, 1966 from Mr. Jón Pálsson; born 1887 in Ólafsfjörður, northern Iceland;

arrived in Canada in 1894; farmer.

For comparative published materials see: Ó.D., II, 225.

C.C.F.C.S. Einarsson Collection: MU-B-8. 388.

10) Recorded from Mrs. Svanfríður Holm. See note no. 2, above.

This item was sung, spontaneously, by Mrs. Holm. She and her husband Gunnlaugur (see note no. 7, above) are both lovers of music and frequently burst into song at the slightest provocation. Most of the verses and rhymes in their repertoire are sung to a small handful of traditional and popular tunes (kn own as <u>stemmur</u>, plural; <u>stemma</u>, singular), selected, seemingly, at random and on the spur of the moment.

This verse describes a journey to the district trading post, traditionally visited (on long caravans of horses) in spring and autumn. Special treats bought for the children included such things as raisins and crystal-formed barley sugar.

C.C.F.C.S. Einarsson Collection: MU-B-36. 1739.

11) Recorded from Mr. Jón Pálsson. See note no. 9, above.

Riding horses were the primary means of travel in Iceland well into the final quarter of the nineteenth century. Horses, women and drink are some of the most popular subjects of traditional Icelandic poetry. Well-to-do farmers would give or 'gift' their children a promising foal at a relatively early age to look after, and later, to ride—the boys in an 'English' saddle, and the girls in a <u>söðull</u>, or side-saddle.

For comparative published materials see: B.P., 886.

C.C.F.C.S. Einarsson Collection: MU-B-8. 390. In the same collection is a similar item recorded from Mrs. Steinunn Valgarðsson (MU-B-3. 122).

12) Recorded from Mr. Jón Pálsson. See note no. 9, above.

For comparative published materials see: S.S., XV, 25.

C.C.F.C.S. Einarsson Collection: MU-B-8. 387. In the same collection is a similar item recorded from Mr. Gunnar Alexander (MU-B-22. 1107).

13) Recorded near Riverton, Manitoba, August 22, 1967 from Mr. Valdimar Johnson; born 1899 in Vestur-Skaftafellssýsla, southeastern Iceland; arrived in Canada in 1902; worked as a fisherman on Lake Winnipeg until 1945 when he began farming near Riverton.

The informant learned this item from his mother Mrs. Ingidóra Sveinsdóttir Johnson. She was his principal source of Icelandic folklore, but since her death in 1926 he has actively sought to augment his repertoire from neighbors and new arrivals from Iceland. The items published in this collection are all learned from his mother.

C.C.F.C.S. Einarsson Collection: MU-C-6.1 (folio 63-A).

14) Recorded from Mr. Jón Pálsson. See note no 9, above.

For comparative published materials see: J.S., 52.

C.C.F.C.S. Einarsson Collection: MU-B-8. 392.

15) Recorded in the Geysir district, near Arborg, Manitoba, August 31, 1966 from Mrs. Steinunn Gísladóttir Bjarnason; born 1887 in Skagafjorður, northern Iceland; arrived in Canada in 1920; farmed with husband in the Geysir district.

C.C.F.C.S. Einarsson Collection: MU-B-9. 450.

16) Recorded from Mr. Valdimar Johnson. See note no. 13, above.

For comparative published materials see: Ó.D., IV, 217; Ó.J.Ó., 39-41; S.S., XV, 44; B.P., 608.

C.C.F.C.S. Einarsson Collection: MU-B-26. 1246.

17) Recorded in Blaine, Washington, August 6, 1969 from Mrs. Dagbjort Elíasdóttir Kjærnested Vopnfjörð; born 1878 in Hnappadalssýsla, western Iceland; arrived in Canada in 1881; housewife. Her youth was spent in New Iceland, Manitoba. She moved with her husband to Winnipeg in 1910, and to the West Coast in 1930. She is now blind.

The informant learned this when she was about five years of age. She refers to it as a langloka (= rigmarole). She has taught it to her children.

The word belja, in line 3, is a verb, meaning to moo or bellow, but it is also a noun commonly used for 'cow'.

For comparative published materials see: Ó. D., IV, 206-207.

C.C.F.C.S. Einarsson Collection: MU-B-33. 1494.

18) Received in a letter from Mrs. Sigurveig Sveinsson. See note no. 6, above.

For comparative published materials see: Ó. D., IV, 283.

C.C.F.C.S. Einarsson Collection: MU-C-6.1 (folio 19, item no. 1).

19) Recorded from Mrs. Steinunn Bjarnason. See note no. 15, above.

Many of the names are nonsensical.

For comparative published materials see: Ó.D., IV, 196; Ó.J.Ó., 19-24; S.S., XV, 46.

C.C.F.C.S. Einarsson Collection: MU-B-9. 451. In the same collection are various parts of the same item recorded from Mrs. Fríða Filipsson (MU-B-34. 1632), and from Mrs. Herdís Eiríksson (MU-B-6. 278).

20) Recorded from Mrs. Sigurveig Sveinsson. See note no. 6, above.

For comparative materials see note no. 19, above.

C.C.F.C.S. Einarsson Collection: MU-C-6.1 (folio 14, item no. 2).

21) Recorded from Mrs. Sigríður Björnsson. See note no. 3, above.

For comparative materials see: AT 2010A and B (The Twelve Days [Gifts] of Christmas), and Ó.D., IV, 298.

C.C.F.C.S. Einarsson Collection: MU-B-2. 55.

22) Recorded from Mrs. Sigríður Björnsson. See note no. 3, above.

The informant, who is blind, recites these rhymes for her own, private amusement, but she has occasionally recited them for nephews and nieces.

For comparative published materials see: Ó.D., IV, 292-294. This text compares in some degree with several of the cumulative tales listed in the Arne-Thompson Index, such as: AT 2015 (The Goat who would not Leave the Hazel Bush), AT 2030 (The Old Woman and her Pig), and AT 2030B* (Pulling the Needle out of the Seamstress's Hand).

C.C.F.C.S. Einarsson Collection: MU-B-2. 62.

23)   Recorded near Mozart, Saskatchewan, June 21, 1967 from Mr. Sigmundur Hjálmarsson Helgason; born 1906 in Leslie, Saskatchewan; farms near Mozart.

Mr. Helgason has taught this cumulative tale to his grandson, in English.

This item bears some similarity to AT 2044 (Pulling up the Turnip).

C.C.F.C.S. Einarsson Collection: MU-B-18. 928.

24)   Recorded in Arborg, Manitoba, August 25, 1966 from Mrs. Herdís Kristjánsdóttir Eiríksson; born 1896 in Fnjóskadalur, northern Iceland; arrived in Canada in 1909; housewife.

The informant remembers that as a newcomer from Iceland she was frequently asked to look after neighbors' children, and that she was often called upon to entertain them with stories and rhymes of this sort that she had learned as a young child in Iceland.

This rhyme, or cumulative tale, bears, again, some similarity to AT 2044 (Pulling up the Turnip).

C.C.F.C.S. Einarsson Collection: MU-B-6. 277.

25)   Recorded in Vancouver, British Columbia, August 9, 1969 from Mr. Jón Hávarðsson Howardson; born 1885 in eastern Iceland; arrived in Canada in 1888; worked as a farmer and fisherman around Siglunes, Manitoba, and, since 1939, as a carpenter in Vancouver.

According to the informant this was the first time since childhood that he had recited this and the other similar 'nursery' rhymes in his repertoire. This is especially noteworthy because, he says, that for a period of twenty years, in mid-life, he almost totally forgot how to speak Icelandic.

For comparative published materials see: Ó.D., IV, 214-215; and S.S., XV, 45.

C.C.F.C.S. Einarsson Collection: MU-B-34. 1636. In the same collection is a similar item recorded from Mrs. Herdís Eiríksson (MU-B-26. 1238).

26) Recorded in Mountain, North Dakota, September 5, 1966 from Mrs. Þórey Björnsson; born 1887 in Skagafjörður, northern Iceland; arrived in Canada in 1907; farmed most of her life with husband near Cavalier, North Dakota.

The mock-heroic tone in this rhyme is largely achieved by including a number of <u>kenningar</u> or elaborate poetical circumlocutions, and <u>heiti</u>, poetical names, which are usually found in ancient scaldic poetry, and <u>rímur</u>, the metrical romances of later centuries which recount the adventures of various heroes of Icelandic and continental myth, legend and history.

For comparative published materials see: S.S., XV, 41.

C.C.F.C.S. Einarsson Collection: MU-B-14. 711.

27) Recorded from Mr. Jón Howardson. See note no. 25, above.

Freyja, among other things, is the Norse goddess of fertility.

For comparative published materials see: Ó.D., IV, 181; Ó.J.Ó., 131-135; and S.S., XV, 42.

C.C.F.C.S. Einarsson Collection: MU-B-34. 1634. In the same collection are similar items recorded from Mrs. Sigríður Björnsson (MU-B-2. 79), Mrs. Herdís Eiríksson (MU-B-26. 1226), Mrs. Fríða Filipsson (MU-B-34. 1649), Mrs. Ásrún Johnson (MU-B-34. 1628), and Mr. Lárus Nordal (MU-B-11. 490).

28) Recorded near Arborg, Manitoba, August 28, 1966 from Mrs. Guðrún Helgadóttir Pálsson; born in Mýrasýsla, midwestern Iceland in 1895; arrived in North Dakota in 1900, and in Manitoba in 1901; farms with husband in Geysir district near Arborg.

For comparative published materials see: S.S., XV, 39-40.

C.C.F.C.S. Einarsson Collection: MU-B-9. 411.

29) Recorded from Mrs. Hrund Skúlason. See note no. 1, above.

For comparative published materials see: Ó.D., IV, 212.

C.C.F.C.S. Einarsson Collection: MU-B-44. 2280.

30) Recorded in Mozart, Saskatchewan, June 19, 1967 from Mrs. Jóhanna Stefánsdóttir Sölvason; born 1873 in Skagafjörður, northern

Iceland; arrived in North Dakota in 1899, and five years later in Saskatchewan; farmed with her husband near Wynyard, Saskatchewan.

The first eleven lines of this rhyme were recorded on tape, the remaining nine were recorded in my field notes.

For comparative materials see: Ó.D., IV, 384; and S.S., XV, 38-39.

C.C.F.C.S. Einarsson Collection: MU-B-6. 823, and MU-C-6.1 (folio 28, item 1). In the same collection is a similar item recorded from Mrs. Hrund Skúlason (MU-B-44. 2270).

31) Recorded from Mr. Valdimar Johnson. See note no. 13, above.

For comparative published materials see: H.Á., 6; and Ó.D., IV, 304.

C.C.F.C.S. Einarsson Collection: MU-B-26. 1253.

32) Recorded in Wynyard, Saskatchewan, June 26, 1967 from Mr. Waldimar Jónsson Johnson; born in 1874 in Mývatnssveit, northern Iceland; arrived in Canada in 1893. He has farmed near Wynyard since 1905. In his spare time he writes poetry and composes music.

C.C.F.C.S. Einarsson Collection: MU-C-6.1 (folio 51-A, item 1).

33) Recorded in Gimli, Manitoba, August 23, 1966 from Mr. Lárus Bjarni Rafnsson Nordal; born in 1879 in Akranes, southwestern Iceland; arrived in Canada in 1900; farmed near Leslie, Saskatchewan for thirty-two years, and then moved to Gimli where, before his retirement, he worked as a carpenter. He is a published poet.

C.C.F.C.S. Einarsson Collection: MU-B-11. 492.

34) Recorded from Mr. Valdimar Johnson. See note no. 13, above.

For comparative published materials see: H.Á., 14; Ó.D., IV, 307; and, in an adapted format, J.Ó, 161.

C.C.F.C.S. Einarsson Collection: MU-B-26. 1262.

35) Recorded in Arnes, Manitoba, August 22, 1967 from Mrs. Jóhanna Sumarliðadóttir Thorkelsson; born 1893 in Miðfjörður, northern Iceland; arrived in Canada in 1901; farmed with husband near Arnes.

For comparative published materials see: Ó.D., IV, 305; and S.N., 246.

C.C.F.C.S. Einarsson Collection: MU-B-26. 1271. In the same collection is an item recorded from Mr. Valdimar Johnson (MU-B-26. 1258).

36) Recorded from Mrs. Sigríður Björnsson. See note no. 3, above.

For comparative published materials see: H.Á., 19; and Ó.D., IV, 309.

C.C.F.C.S. Einarsson Collection: MU-B-2. 110. In the same collection is a similar item recorded from Mr. Valdimar Johnson (MU-B-26. 1255).

37) Received in a letter from Mrs. Sigurveig Sveinsson. See note no. 6, above.

For comparative published materials see: H.Á., 8.

C.C.F.C.S. Einarsson Collection: MU-C-6.1 (folio 21, item no. 3).

38) Received in a letter from Mrs. Sigurveig Sveinsson. See note no. 6, above.

For comparative published materials see: H.Á., 11.

C.C.F.C.S. Einarsson Collection: MU-C-6.1 (folio 21, item no. 4).

39) Received in a letter from Mrs. Sigurveig Sveinsson. See note no. 6, above.

For comparative published materials see: H.Á. 18; and Ó.D., IV, 308.

C.C.F.C.S. Einarsson Collection: MU-C-6.1 (folio 20, item no. 4).

40) Recorded from Mrs. Sigríður Björnsson. See note no. 3, above.

For comparative published materials see: H.Á. 18; and Ó.D., IV, 308.

C.C.F.C.S. Einarsson Collection: MU-B-2. 108. In the same collection is a similar item recorded from Mrs. Jóhanna Thorkelsson (MU-B-26. 1270).

41) Recorded from Mr. Valdimar Johnson. See note no. 13, above.

For comparative published materials see: Ó.D., IV, 306.

C.C.F.C.S. Einarsson Collection: MU-B-26. 1261.

42)	Recorded from Mr. Valdimar Johnson. See note no. 13, above.

For comparative published materials see: H.Á., 26; and Ó.D., IV, 312.

C.C.F.C.S. Einarsson Collection: MU-B-26. 1254.

43)	Recorded from Mr. Lárus Nordal. See note no. 33, above.

For comparative published materials see: H.Á., 6; and Ó.D., IV, 305.

C.C.F.C.S. Einarsson Collection: MU-B-11. 493 and 511. In the same collection is a similar item recorded from Mrs. Sigríður Björnsson (MU-B-2. 109).

44)	Recorded from Mr. Valdimar Johnson. See note no. 13, above.

For comparative published materials see: H.Á., 19; and Ó.D., IV, 309.

C.C.F.C.S. Einarsson Collection: MU-B-26. 1257.

45)	Recorded from Mr. Valdimar Johnson. See note no. 13, above.

C.C.F.C.S. Einarsson Collection: MU-C-6.1 (folio 51-B, item no. 1).

46)	Recorded from Mr. Lárus Nordal. See note no. 33, above.

For comparative published materials see: H.Á., 10; Ó.D., IV, 306; and B.P., 833.

C.C.F.C.S. Einarsson Collection: MU-B-11. 512.

47/48)	Recorded near Hnausa, Manitoba, September 4, 1969 from Mr. Andrés Guðbjartsson; born 1897 in Barðastrandasýsla, western Iceland; arrived in Canada in 1911; left again for Iceland in 1916, and returned to Canada in 1921; farms near Riverton. The principal informant of these two items is the wife of Andrés, Elísabet Elíasdóttir; born in western Iceland; arrived in Canada with her husband in 1921.

For comparative published materials to item no. 47 see: H.Á., 22; and Ó.D., IV, 311. Item no. 48 is the same as item no. 40, above, except for one word in the last line which, as the translation reveals, has been interpreted differently by Mrs. Guðbjartsson.

C.C.F.C.S. Einarsson Collection: MU-B-42. 2173 and 2174.

Notes

49) Recorded from Mr. Valdimar Johnson, August 24, 1967. See note no. 13, above.

For comparative published materials see: J.Á./Ó.D., I, 16.

C.C.F.C.S. Einarsson Collection: MU-B-28. 1317.

50) Recorded from Mr. Valdimar Johnson, August 24, 1967 See note no. 13, above.

For comparative published materials see: J.Á./Ó.D., I, 19.

C.C.F.C.S. Einarsson Collection: MU-B-28. 1319.

51) Received in a letter from Mrs. Sigurveig Sveinsson. See note no. 6, above.

The number "eight" refers to four horseshoes on four feet. The number "twenty" signifies the five nails in each horseshoe. The "extra one", i.e. extra head, refers to the head of the horse as opposed to the head of a nail.

For comparative published materials see: J.Á./Ó.D., I, 20.

C.C.F.C.S. Einarsson Collection: MU-C-6.1 (folio 17, item no. 3).

52) Recorded from Mr. Valdimar Johnson. See note no. 13, above.

For comparative published materials see: J.Á./Ó.D., I, 31.

C.C.F.C.S. Einarsson Collection: MU-B-26. 1243.

53) Recorded in field notes from Mrs. Jóhanna Sölvason. See note no. 30, above.

For comparative published materials see: J.Á./Ó.D., I, 31.

C.C.F.C.S. Einarsson Collection: MU-C-6.1 (folio 24, item no. 1). In the same collection is a similar item received in a letter from Mrs. Sigurveig Sveinsson, MU-C-6.1 (folio 17, item no. 2).

54) Recorded from Mrs. Jóhanna Thorkelsson. See note no. 35, above.

For comparative published materials see: J.Á./Ó.D., I, 45; and S.S., XVI, 19.

C.C.F.C.S. Einarsson Collection: MU-B-26. 1277.

55) Recorded from Mrs. Jóhanna Thorkelsson. See note no. 35, above.

For comparative published materials see: J.Á./Ó.D., I, 46; and S.S., XVI, 21.

C.C.F.C.S. Einarsson Collection: MU-B-26. 1276.

56) Recorded in Vancouver, British Columbia, August 12, 1969 from Friðfinnur Júlíus Ólafsson Lyngdal; born 1880 near Eyjafjörður, northern Iceland; arrived in Canada in 1904; farmed near Lake Manitoba, then became a merchant in Gimli, Manitoba. He moved to Vancouver in 1938 where, until his retirement, he kept a store.

For comparative published materials see: J.Á./Ó.D., I, 46.

C.C.F.C.S. Einarsson Collection: MU-B-36. 1890.

57) Recorded from Mrs. Jóhanna Thorkelsson. See note no. 35, above. The riddle describes the face of a cat.

For comparative published materials see: J.Á./Ó.D., I, 48.

C.C.F.C.S. Einarsson Collection: MU-B-26. 1267.

58) Recorded in Mountain, North Dakota, September 6, 1966 from Mr. Guðmundur Júlíus Jónasson; born 1887 in Skagafjörður, northern Iceland; arrived in 1905. He has farmed most of his life near Mountain. He is a published poet.

For comparative published materials see: J.Á./Ó.D., I, 48.

C.C.F.C.S. Einarsson Collection: MU-B-14. 716. In the same collection are similar items recorded from Mr. Sigmundur Helgason (MU-B-18. 927), from Mrs. Dómhildur Johnson (MU-B-15. 766), and from Mr. Valdimar Johnson (MU-B-26. 1249).

59) Recorded near Elfros, Saskatchewan, June 23, 1967 from Mr. Helgi Jónsson Hornfjörð; born 1897 in the Ísafold district north of Riverton, Manitoba; farms near Elfros.

For comparative published materials see: S.S., XVI, 24.

C.C.F.C.S. Einarsson Collection: MU-B-18. 944.

60) Recorded from Mrs. Jóhanna Thorkelsson. See note no. 35, above.

For comparative published materials see: J.Á./Ó.D., I, 56; and S.S.,

XVI, 25. Both Árnason and Sigfússon offer 'basket' as the solution.

C.C.F.C.S. Einarsson Collection: MU-B-26. 1279.

61) Recorded from Mrs. Jóhanna Thorkelsson. See note no. 35, above.

For comparative published materials see: J.Á./Ó.D., I, 101.

C.C.F.C.S. Einarsson Collection: MU-B-26. 1278.

62) Recorded in Wynyard, Saskatchewan, June 16, 1967 from Mrs. Dómhildur Jóhannsdóttir Johnson; born 1878 in Vopnafjörður, eastern Iceland; arrived in Canada in 1909. She has been a housewife in Wynyard since her arrival.

For comparative published materials see: J.Á./Ó.D., I, 57.

C.C.F.C.S. Einarsson Collection: MU-B-15. 765. In the same collection is a similar item recorded from Mr. Valdimar Johnson (MU-B-28. 1318).

63) Recorded from Mr. Valdimar Johnson. See note no. 13, above.

Hel, in Norse mythology, is the abode of the dead.

For comparative published materials see: J.Á./Ó.D., I, 57; and S.S., XVI, 22.

C.C.F.C.S. Einarsson Collection: MU-B-26. 1244. In the same collection is a similar item recorded from Mr. Jón Mýrdal (MU-B-34. 1592).

64) Recorded in the Geysir district, near Arborg, Manitoba, August, 1967 from Mrs. Olga Egilsdóttir Hólm Pálsson; born 1919 near Arborg; farms with husband in the Geysir district.

For comparative published materials see: J.Á./Ó.D., I, 60; and S.S., XVI, 20.

C.C.F.C.S. Einarsson Collection: MU-B-26. 1179. In the same collection is a similar item recorded from Mr. Valdimar Johnson (MU-B-26. 1248).

65) Recorded in Wynyard, Saskatchewan, August 17, 1967, from Mr. Gísli Gillis; born 1878 in Húnavatnssýsla, northern Iceland; arrived in Canada in 1887; farmed in North Dakota 1902-1922, and then, until his

retirement, near Wynyard.
>For comparative published materials see: J.Á./Ó.D., I, 70.
>C.C.F.C.S. Einarsson Collection: MU-B-16. 858 .1.

66) Recorded from Mr. Valdimar Johnson. See note no. 13, above.
>For comparative published materials see: J.Á./Ó.D., I, 71.
>C.C.F.C.S. Einarsson Collection: MU-B-26. 1242.

67) Recorded in Gardar, North Dakota, September 7, 1966, from Mrs. Svava Gamalíelsdóttir Flanagan; born 1908 near Gardar.
>For comparative published materials see: J.Á./Ó.D., I, 88.
>C.C.F.C.S. Einarsson Collection: MU-B-14. 719.

68) Recorded from Mr. Jón Mýrdal. See note no. 5, above.
>For comparative published materials see: J.Á./Ó.D., I, 95.
>C.C.F.C.S. Einarsson Collection: MU-B-34. 1593.

69) Recorded from Mr. Valdimar Johnson, August 24, 1967. See note no. 13, above.
>For comparative published materials see: J.Á./Ó.D., I, 103; and S.S., XVI, 28.
>C.C.F.C.S. Einarsson Collection: MU-B-28. 1321.

70) Recorded from Mr. Valdimar Johnson, August 24, 1967. See note no. 13, above.
>For comparative published materials see: J.Á./Ó.D., I, 108; and S.S., XVI, 26.
>C.C.F.C.S. Einarsson Collection: MU-B-28. 1320.

71) Recorded from Mrs. Jóhanna Thorkelsson. See note no. 35, above.
>For comparative published materials see: J.Á./Ó.D., I, 110.
Árnason's solution is as follows: A woman eats while breastfeeding a child while sitting on a mare eating grass while giving suck to her foal.
>C.C.F.C.S. Einarsson Collection: MU-B-26. 1269.

Notes

72) Recorded from Mr. Jón Howardson, August 12, 1969. See note no. 25, above.

For comparative published materials see: S.H., 33.

C.C.F.C.S. Einarsson Collection: MU-B-36. 1738. 14.

73) Recorded in field notes from Mrs. Jóhanna Sölvason. See note no. 30, above.

C.C.F.C.S. Einarsson Collection: MU-C-6.1 (folio 24, item no. 3).

74) Recorded from Mrs. Sigríður Björnsson. See note no. 3, above.

C.C.F.C.S. Einarsson Collection: MU-B-2. 82.

75) Recorded from Mrs. Jóhanna Thorkelsson. See note no. 35, above.

For comparative published materials see: J.Á./Ó.D., I, 122; and S.S., XVI, 13.

C.C.F.C.S. Einarsson Collection: MU-B-26. 1275. In the same collection is a similar item recorded from Mr. Jón Howardson (MU-B-36. 1738. 13).

76) Recorded from Mrs. Jóhanna Thorkelsson. See note no. 35, above.

For comparative published materials see: J.Á./Ó.D., I, 124. Árnason's solution is as follows: A man sits on a three-legged stool holding a bone which a dog takes out of his hand. The man becomes angry and hits the dog with the stool.

C.C.F.C.S. Einarsson Collection: MU-B-26. 1268.

77) Recorded from Mr. Jón Mýrdal. See note no. 5, above.

C.C.F.C.S. Einarsson Collection: MU-B-34. 1591.

78) Recorded from Mr. Sigmundur Helgason. See note no. 23, above.

C.C.F.C.S. Einarsson Collection: MU-B-18. 926.

79) Recorded from Mr. Valdimar Johnson. See note no. 13, above.

For comparative published materials see: J.Á./Ó.D., I, 126.

C.C.F.C.S. Einarsson Collection: MU-B-26. 1245.

80) Recorded from Mr. Friðfinnur Lyngdal. See note no. 56, above.
C.C.F.C.S. Einarsson Collection: MU-B-36. 1892.

81) Recorded from Mr. Friðfinnur Lyngdal. See note no. 56, above.
C.C.F.C.S. Einarsson Collection: MU-B-36. 1891.

82) Recorded from Mr. Valdimar Johnson. See note no. 13, above.
C.C.F.C.S. Einarsson Collection: MU-C-6.1 (folio 200, item no. 1).

83) Recorded from Mrs. Hrund Skúlason. See note no. 1, above.
For comparative published materials see: Ó.D., II, 184.
C.C.F.C.S. Einarsson Collection: MU-B-44. 2271.

84) Recorded from Mrs. Hrund Skúlason. See note no. 1, above.
For comparative published materials see: Ó.D., II, 324.
C.C.F.C.S. Einarsson Collection: MU-B-44. 2272.

85) Received in a letter from Mrs. Sigurveig Sveinsson. See note no. 6, above.
For comparative published materials see: S.S., XVI, 39.
C.C.F.C.S. Einarsson Collection: MU-C-6.1 (folio 14, item no. 3).

86) Received in a letter from Mrs. Sigurveig Sveinsson. See note no. 6, above.
C.C.F.C.S. Einarsson Collection: MU-C-6.1 (folio 14, item no. 4).

87) Recorded in Lundar, Manitoba, July, 1967, from Mr. Hjörtur Hjartarson; born 1908 in southwestern Iceland; arrived in Canada in 1913; farms near Lundar.

Mr. Hjartarson learned this item when he was a small boy from one of his parents.

For comparative published materials see: Ó.D., IV, 111-118. Some variants of this rhyme have ninety verses.

C.C.F.C.S. Einarsson Collection: MU-B-21. 1077. In the same collection are similar items recorded from Mrs. Steinunn Bjarnason (MU-B-9. 445), and from Mrs. Fríða Holm (MU-B-35. 1697).

Notes 335

88) Recorded from Mrs. Þórey Björnsson. See note no. 26, above.

Mrs. Björnsson, whose mother left for Canada when Mrs. Björnsson was one year old, stayed in Iceland with her mother's sister from whom she learned this rhyme. Mrs. Björnsson emigrated to Canada with her father when she was twenty years old. Asked whether or not she had believed in the figure of Grýla, Mrs. Björnsson said, "Sure. Krakkarnir, þau voru hrædd við þetta ferlíki." (= Sure. The kids, they were afraid of this monster.)

C.C.F.C.S. Einarsson Collection: MU-B-14. 712.

89) Recorded from Mrs. Jóhanna Thorkelsson. See note no. 35, above.

For comparative published materials see: J.P.G., 298.

C.C.F.C.S. Einarsson Collection: MU-B-26. 1272.

90) Recorded in Arborg, Manitoba, August 26, 1966 from Miss Margrét Bjarnason; born 1902 in Winnipeg; farmed with her twin brother, Björn Bjarnason, on family homestead for many years before moving into Arborg.

This item was sung by Miss Bjarnason which is somewhat unusual for this genre, but not unknown. Mrs. Fríða Holm also put a melody to one of these rhymes.

For comparative published materials see: B.P., 654-655, and 659.

C.C.F.C.S. Einarsson Collection: MU-B-10. 463.

91) Recorded from Mrs. Sigríður Björnsson. See note no. 3, above.

For comparative published materials see: J.Á., I, 207; Ó.D., IV, 146; and S.S., XV, 32.

C.C.F.C.S. Einarsson Collection: MU-B-2. 76. In the same collection are similar items recorded from Mr. Jón Howardson (MU-B-34. 1641) and Mrs. Hrund Skúlason (MU-B-44. 2276). Mr. Howardson says he learned rhymes of this sort from some of the older Icelandic men that he used to work with in lumbering and fishing camps. Unlike Mrs. Þórey Björnsson, who was raised in Iceland (see note no 26), he says he was never frightened, as a child, by rhymes or stories about Grýla.

92) Recorded from Mrs. Fríða Holm. See note no. 2, above.

For comparative published materials see: J.Á., I, 207; Ó.D., IV, 146; and S.S., XV, 32.

C.C.F.C.S. Einarsson Collection: MU-B-34. 1653.

93) Recorded from Mrs. Sigríður Björnsson. See note no. 3, above.

The name Magnús in lines 12 and 13 refers, in this instance, to the collector. It is likely that the genre permits this type of a 'slotting' technique to personalize the rhyme and maximize its scaring effect as required in a given situation. See also item no. 91 where the same informant has inserted her own nickname in the final line.

For comparative published materials see: Ó.D., IV, 111-118. For comparison see item no. 83.

C.C.F.C.S. Einarsson Collection: MU-B-2. 74.

94) Recorded from Mrs. Sigríður Björnsson. See note no. 3, above.

For comparative published materials see: Ó.D., IV, 141, 144; and S.S., XV, 32.

C.C.F.C.S. Einarsson Collection: MU-B-2. 75.

95) Recorded from Mrs. Sigríður Björnsson. See note no. 3, above.

C.C.F.C.S. Einarsson Collection: MU-B-2. 78.

96) Recorded from Mrs. Sigríður Björnsson. See note no. 3, above.

For comparative published materials see: Ó.D., IV, 173.

C.C.F.C.S. Einarsson Collection: MU-B-2. 86.

97) Recorded from Mrs. Sigríður Björnsson. See note no. 3, above.

For comparative published materials see: Ó.D., IV, 172; and S.S., XV, 13.

C.C.F.C.S. Einarsson Collection: MU-B-2. 85.

98) Recorded from Mrs. Sigríður Björnsson. See note no. 3, above.

C.C.F.C.S. Einarsson Collection: MU-B-2. 85.

99) Recorded from Mrs. Sigríður Björnsson. See note no. 3, above.

For comparative published materials see: Ó.D., IV, 164; and S.S.,

XV, 30. According to Daviðsson this is the first verse in a twenty-seven verse poem.

C.C.F.C.S. Einarsson Collection: MU-B-2. 84.

100) Recorded near Arborg, Manitoba, August 26, 1966 from Mr. Kár Simundson; born in the late 1950's in Arborg. He is a student.

For comparative published materials see: Ó.D., IV, 262, and 263.

C.C.F.C.S. Einarsson Collection: MU-B-8. 348.

101) Recorded from Mrs. Sigríður Björnsson. See note no. 3, above.

For comparative published materials see: Ó.D., IV, 267; and S.S., XV, 13.

C.C.F.C.S. Einarsson Collection: MU-B-2. 89.

102) Recorded from Mrs. Sigríður Björnsson. See note no. 3, above.

For comparative published materials see: S.S., XV, 12.

C.C.F.C.S. Einarsson Collection: MU-B-2. 88.

103) Recorded from Mr. Waldimar Johnson. See note no. 32, above.

For comparative published materials see: S.S., XV, 12.

C.C.F.C.S. Einarsson Collection: MU-B-19. 959.

104) Recorded in Gimli, Manitoba, August 21, 1966 from Mr. Þórður Bjarnason; born in 1902 in Arnes, Manitoba; farmer and fisherman.

For comparative published materials see: Ó.D., IV, 267.

C.C.F.C.S. Einarsson Collection: MU-B-3. 127.

105) Recorded from Mrs. Sigríður Björnsson. See note no. 3, above.

The word hrip (= crib) in the last line refers not to a child's crib but a crib-like box used for carrying fuel or fodder either singly on a man's back or as one of a pair across the back of a horse. The incident that inspired the verse is no longer known. This item may originally have been intended as a mock lullaby, but has, over time, entered oral tradition as the genuine article.

For comparative published materials see: B.P., 669.

C.C.F.C.S. Einarsson Collection: MU-B-2. 71.

106) Recorded in Vancouver, British Columbia, August 10, 1969 from Mrs. Helga Sigtryggsdóttir Howardsson; born in early 1920's near Kandahar, Saskatchewan; housewife.

For comparative published materials see: B.P., 832.

C.C.F.C.S. Einarsson Collection: MU-B-35. 1682.

107) Recorded in Arborg, Manitoba, August 31, 1969 from Mr. Björn Bjarnason; born 1902 in Winnipeg. He farmed for many years with his twin sister, Margrét Bjarnason (see note no. 90, above) on the family homestead before moving into Arborg where he works as a carpenter. He has participated in many community theatre productions and is an excellent storyteller and mimic.

This item was recited in priestly, incantorial tones. A favorite target of Mr. Bjarnason's humour is Lutheran 'superstition.' He himself is a Unitarian.

C.C.F.C.S. Einarsson Collection: MU-B-41. 2114. In the same collection is a similar item recorded from Mrs. Sigríður Björnsson (MU-B-2. 59).

108) Recorded from Mrs. Sigríður Björnsson. See note no. 3, above.

C.C.F.C.S. Einarsson Collection: MU-B-2. 58.

109) Received in a letter from Mrs. Sigurveig Sveinsson. See note no. 6, above.

C.C.F.C.S. Einarsson Collection: MU-C-6.1 (folio 16, item no. 3).

110) Recorded from Mrs. Sigríður Björnsson. See note no. 3, above.

C.C.F.C.S. Einarsson Collection: MU-C-6.1 (folio 77, item no. 1).

111) Recorded from Mrs. Sigurveig Sveinsson. See note no. 6, above.

C.C.F.C.S. Einarsson Collection: MU-C-6.1 (folio 15, item no. 5).

112) Recorded from Mrs. Sigurveig Sveinsson. See note no. 6, above.

C.C.F.C.S. Einarsson Collection: MU-C-6.1 (folio 12, item no. 2).

113) Recorded from Mr. Páll Hallson. See note no. 8, above.

The verse was sung by Mr. Hallson.

C.C.F.C.S. Einarsson Collection: MU-B-1.3.

114) Recorded from Mrs. Jóhanna Thorkelsson. See note no. 35, above.

This verse was sung by Mrs. Thorkelsson.

C.C.F.C.S. Einarsson Collection: MU-B-26. 1283.

115) Recorded from Mr. Páll Hallson. See note no. 8, above.

Mr. Hallson sang the verse.

For comparative published materials see: Skírnir, LXXXIX, 310.

C.C.F.C.S. Einarsson Collection: MU-B-1. 2. In the same collection is a similar item recorded from Mr. Jón Howardson (MU-B-36. 1738 .16).

116) Recorded from Mr. Björn Bjarnason, August 26, 1966. See note no. 107, above.

Mr. Bjarnason sang this verse.

C.C.F.C.S. Einarsson Collection: MU-B-6. 291. In the same collection is a similar item recorded from Rev. Albert Kristjánsson (MU-B-34. 1619).

117) Recorded from Mr. Björn Bjarnason, August 25, 1966. See note no. 107, above.

This verse is from a mock-heroic epic poem of great length. Mr. Bjarnason sang this verse mimicking the voice and manner of his friend Mr. Tímoteus Böðvarsson (see note no. 119, below) who has a deep and powerful singing voice.

For comparative published materials see: V.Á., 39.

C.C.F.C.S. Einarsson Collection: MU-B-11. 570.

118) Recorded from Mrs. Jóhanna Thorkelsson. See note no. 35, above.

Mrs. Thorkelsson sang this verse.

C.C.F.C.S. Einarsson Collection: MU-B-26. 1284.

119) Recorded in Gimli, Manitoba, July 15, 1967, from Mr. Tímoteus Böðvarsson; born 1885 in Mýrasýsla, southwestern Iceland; arrived in Canada in 1905; farmer and postmaster for the Geysir district near Arborg. He was very active in local theatre productions in his younger days.

Mr. Böðvarsson sang this verse.

C.C.F.C.S. Einarsson Collection: MU-B-22. 100.

120) Recorded from Mrs. Jóhanna Thorkelsson. See note no. 35, above.

This verse was sung by Mrs. Thorkelsson.

C.C.F.C.S. Einarsson Collection: MU-B-26. 1282. In the same collection is a similar item recorded from Mrs. Ragna Baldvinsson (MU-B-4. 203).

121) Recorded from Mr. Andrés Guðbjartsson, August 27, 1966. See note no. 47/48, above.

This item was sung by Mr. Guðbjartsson. He says he learned this and similar songs in the seaside villages of the western fjords of Iceland. He says, „Þetta eru rallvísur úr landi." (= These are 'on-the-town' shoreleave songs.

C.C.F.C.S. Einarsson Collection: MU-B-7. 318.

122) Recorded from Mr. Andrés Guðbjartsson. See note no. 47/48, above.

This item was sung by Mr. Guðbjartsson.

C.C.F.C.S. Einarsson Collection: MU-B-7. 314.

123) Recorded from Mr. Hjörtur Hjartarson. See note no. 87, above.

C.C.F.C.S. Einarsson Collection: MU-C-6.1 (folio 37, item no. 1).

124) Recorded from Mr. Gunnlaugur Holm, August 9, 1969. See note no. 7, above.

This item was sung by Mr. Holm to the tune of "Comin' Thro' the Rye," a Scottish folksong.

C.C.F.C.S. Einarsson Collection: MU-B-35. 1672.

125) Recorded from Mr. Andrés Guðbjartsson, August 27, 1966. See note no. 47/48, above.

Asked where he learned this and other similar songs, Mr. Guðbjartsson's comment was: „Þetta sungu þeir á sjónum." (= They sang this at sea.).

C.C.F.C.S. Einarsson Collection: MU-B-7. 316.

126) Recorded in Gimli, Manitoba, August 22, 1966 from Mrs. Þórunn Anderson; born 1885 in Vopnafjörður, eastern Iceland; arrived in Canada

in her late teens or early twenties; housewife.

This item was sung by Mrs. Anderson. She knew a number of dance songs that she learned at dances and parties in Vopnafjörður before she emigrated.

C.C.F.C.S. Einarsson Collection: MU-B-5. 217.

127) Recorded from Mr. Valdimar Johnson, August 24, 1967. See note no. 13, above.

This item was sung by Mr. Johnson.

C.C.F.C.S. Einarsson Collection: MU-B-28. 1323.

128) Recorded from Mrs. Sigríður Björnsson. See note no. 3, above.

This item was sung by Mrs. Björnsson at the collector's request. She was reluctant to sing because she said she had difficulty in carrying a tune.

C.C.F.C.S. Einarsson Collection: MU-B-2. 101.

129) Recorded in Arborg, Manitoba, August 28, 1966 from Mrs. Guðrún Magnússon; born during the 1890's in Grindavík, southwestern Iceland; arrived in Canada as a young woman.

Mrs. Magnússon sang this item. She learned it in Grindavík at dances. The music was usually supplied by Magnús of Hraun playing a concertina.

C.C.F.C.S. Einarsson Collection: MU-B-7. 339.

130) Recorded from Mrs. Þórunn Anderson, August 21, 1967. See note no. 126, above.

This item was sung by Mrs. Anderson.

C.C.F.C.S. Einarsson Collection: MU-B-26. 1240.

131) Recorded from Mr. Valdimar Johnson, August 24, 1967. See note no. 13, above.

The reference in the third line is to a horn spoon. These were often elaborately carved with the owner's name.

C.C.F.C.S. Einarsson Collection: MU-B-28. 1325. 2.

132) Recorded in Gimli, Manitoba from Mrs. Ingibjörg Guðmundsdóttir Bjarnason; born 1902 in Eyjafjörður, northern Iceland; arrived in Canada

in 1913; housewife in Gimli.

    This item was sung by Mrs. Bjarnason.

    C.C.F.C.S. Einarsson Collection: MU-B-3. 139.

133) Recorded from Mr. Björn Bjarnason, August 25, 1966. See note no. 107, above.

    This item was sung by Mr. Bjarnason.

    C.C.F.C.S. Einarsson Collection: MU-B-6. 259.

134) Recorded from Mr. Jón Howardson. See note no. 25, above.

    Asked where he learned this poem and others like it, Mr. Howardson replied: „Sumt úr bókum, og sumt heyrði ég eftir öðrum. Ég var, þó ég segji sjálfur frá, þá var ég næmur á svona þegar ég var ungur." (= Some from books and some I learned from others. I had, even if I say so myself, a talent for this sort of thing when I was young.)

    Mr. Howardson lost his wife in 1924, left his farm and began living among the 'English' and all but lost his mastery of Icelandic, which he then had to relearn in later life. Much of his repertoire is from this re-entry period, but the rest is a part of his childhood memories that survived his temporary loss of the Icelandic language.

    C.C.F.C.S. Einarsson Collection: MU-B-34. 1638.

135) Recorded from Mrs. Jóhanna Thorkelsson. See note no. 35, above.

    For comparative published materials see: G.J., VII, 140.

    C.C.F.C.S. Einarsson Collection: MU-B-26. 1274.

136) Recorded from Mr. Valdimar Johnson, August 24, 1967. See note no. 13, above.

    This poem was sung by Mr. Johnson. He calls it "Sinforianus," but says he doesn't think that's the actual title. He learned the poem from his mother.

    C.C.F.C.S. Einarsson Collection: MU-B-28. 1322.

137) Recorded on Hecla Island, Manitoba, August 26, 1966 from Mrs. Sigþóra Þorláksdóttir Tómasson; born 1892 in Vopnafjörður, eastern

Iceland; arrived in Canada in 1905; housewife and operator of the telephone exchange on Hecla.

Mrs. Tómasson learned the poem when she was seven years old from her mother. Of the poem she says, „Það er í Biblíunni." (= It's in the Bible.). The poem dates from the seventeenth century.

For comparative published materials see: B.P., 538-39.

C.C.F.C.S. Einarsson Collection: MU-B-7. 295. In the same collection are parts of the same poem recorded from Mrs. Ingibjörg Bjarnason (MU-B-3. 139) who made this comment about the poem, „Mamma sagði það væri eitthvað miðalda kvæði, aftur í fornöld."
(= Mother said it was some medieval poem, from ancient times.) She calls it, „nokkurskonar sögukvæði" (= a sort of a story poem). Mrs. Bjarnason also sang what she knew of this poem, unlike Mrs. Tómasson who recited it. Parts of the poem were also recorded from Mrs. Ragna Baldvinsson (MU-B-4. 204) and Mr. Valdimar Johnson (MU-B-28. 1326).

138)   Recorded in Gimli, Manitoba, July 17, 1967 from Miss Anna Nordal; born 1902 in Winnipeg, Manitoba; nurse; lives with her father, Mr. Lárus Nordal (see note no. 33, above) in Gimli.

GRALLARI is the popular name of an Icelandic Lutheran hymnal (GRADUALE: EIN ALMENNILEG MESSUSÖNGBÓK) which was used in the country's churches from 1594 well into the nineteenth century, at least in some parishes.

This item was sung by Miss Nordal. She learned the poem when she was about six years old from her maternal great aunt when she was over ninety. The poem is probably based on the Biblical passage in Luke 2: 36-37 of the NEW TESTAMENT.

C.C.F.C.S. Einarsson Collection: MU-B-22. 1095.

139)   Recorded from Mr. Björn Bjarnason, August 25, 1966. See note no. 107, above.

This item was sung by Mr. Bjarnason. He learned the poem from his father.

C.C.F.C.S. Einarsson Collection: MU-B-6. 254.

140)   Recorded from Mrs. Guðrún Pálsson. See note no. 28, above.

The poem is by Sirrah Kolbeinn Þorsteinsson (1731-1783), written sometime during the years 1759-1764 when he was a curate to the vicar at Gilsbakki, Sr. Jón Jónsson who was his father-in-law. The poem is a description of the welcome that his daughter Guðrún received from her grandfather, the vicar, upon her return to Gilsbakki. Guðrún was born in 1758. The poem has had a number of names through the years, but the one that seems to be the most popular is „Gilsbakkaþula", (= The Gilsbakki Rigmarole), possibly because of its catalogue quality so common to traditional þulur, or rigmaroles.

For comparative published materials see: <u>Huld</u>, 71.

C.C.F.C.S. Einarsson Collection: MU-B-9. 412. In the same collection are similar items recorded from Mrs. Ingibjörg Renessee (MU-B-11. 533) and Mrs. Steinunn Valgarðsson (MU-B-2. 113). Mrs. Valgarðsson has often recited this poem at birthday parties and other celebrations at the Betel Nursing Home in Gimli, Manitoba.

141)   Recorded from Mrs. Hrund Skúlason. See note no. 1, above.

For comparative material see: AT 2271 (<u>Mock</u> <u>Stories</u> <u>for</u> <u>Children</u>).

C.C.F.C.S. Einarsson Collection: MU-B-44. 2274

142)   Recorded from Mrs. Hrund Skúlason. See note no. 1, above.

For comparative material see: AT2271 (<u>Mock</u> <u>Stories</u> <u>for</u> <u>Children</u>).

C.C.F.C.S. Einarsson Collection: MU-B-44. 2273. 2.

143-285)   Recorded from Mr. Gunnlaugur Holm, August 13, 1969. See note no. 7, above.

In addition to his own repertoire of proverbs and sayings, Mr. Holm made a point of recording those he heard from others, including some, undoubtedly, from English language sources.

For comparative materials see: B.V./Ó.H.

C.C.F.C.S. Einarsson Collection: MU-B-36. 1747-1885. 1.

286-322)   Recorded in field notes from Mr. Valdimar Johnson. See note no. 13, above.

Notes 345

Mr. Johnson's basic proverb repertoire was learned from his mother, but he has added to it from various other sources. Unlike Mr. Holm, he did not have these proverbs written down.

For comparative published materials see: B.V./Ó.H.

C.C.F.C.S. Einarsson Collection: MU-C-6.1 (folio 38, items no. 1-14; and folio 39, items no. 1-23).

323-330) Recorded in the Geysir district near Arborg, Manitoba, August 29, 1966 from Mrs. Indíana Sveinsdóttir Sigurðsson; born 1891 in Skagafjörður, northern Iceland; arrived in Canada in 1906; farms with husband near Arborg.

For comparative published material see: B.V./Ó.H.

C.C.F.C.S. Einarsson Collection: MU-B-8. 396-403.

331) Recorded from Miss Anna Nordal. See note no. 138, above.

For comparative published materials see: B.V./Ó.H.

C.C.F.C.S. Einarsson Collection: MU-B-22. 1097.

332) Recorded in Gimli, Manitoba, August 21, 1966 from Mrs. Steinunn Sigurðardóttir Valgarðsson; born 1867 in Rangárvallasýsla, southern Iceland; arrived in Canada in 1924; housewife.

This type of a formula would usually be employed in a casual and humorous way after the telling of a folktale or a rigmarole or þula.

C.C.F.C.S. Einarsson Collection: MU-B-2. 116.

KEY TO ABBREVIATIONS
IN NOTES

KEY TO ABBREVIATIONS IN NOTES

B.V./Ó.H.   Bjarni Vilhjálmsson and Óskar Halldórsson, ÍSLENZKIR MÁLSHÆTTIR, Reykjavík, 1966.

B.Þ.   Bjarni Þorsteinsson, ÍSLENZK ÞJÓÐLÖG, Copenhagen, 1906-1908.

G.J.   Guðni Jónsson, ÍSLENZKIR SAGNAÞÆTTIR OG ÞJÓÐSÖGUR, 12 vols., Reykjavík, 1957.

H.Á.   Helgi Árnason, ed., HUNDRAÐ OG ÁTTATÍU ÖFUGMÆLAVÍSUR, Reykjavík, 1928.

HULD   HULD, 6 vols. Hannes Þorsteinsson, Jón Thorkelsson, Ólafur Davíðsson, Pálmi Pálsson, Valdimar Ásmundsson, eds., Reykjavík, 1890-98.

J.Á.   Jón Árnason, ÍSLENZKAR ÞJÓÐSÖGUR OG ÆVINTÝRI, 6 vols. Árni Böðvarsson and Bjarni Vilhjálmsson, eds., Reykjavík, 1954-1961.

J.Á./Ó.D.   Jón Árnason and Ólafur Davíðsson, ÍSLENZKAR GÁTUR, SKEMTANIR, VIKIVAKAR OG ÞULUR, 4 vols., Copenhagen, 1887-1903.

J.Ó.   Jón Ólafsson, LJÓÐMÆLI: 1886-1893, Reykjavík, 1896.

J.S.   Jóhann Sveinsson, ed., ÉG SKAL KVEÐA VIÐ ÞIG VEL, Reykjavík, 1947.

J.Þ.G.   Jón Þorláksson Guðmundsson in: SNÓT: NOKKUR KVÆÐI EPTIR ÝMISS SKÁLD, 2nd. ed., Reykjavík, 1865.

Ó.D.   See: J.Á./Ó.D., above.

Ó.J.Ó.   Ófeigur J. Ófeigsson, ed., „RAULA ÉG VIÐ ROKKINN MINN ": ÞULUR OG ÞJÓÐKVÆÐI, Reykjavík, 1945.

S.H. Snorri Hjartarson, Gísli Gestsson and Páll Jónsson, eds., HEIMAN ÉG FÓR: VASALESBÓK, Reykjavík, 1946.

SKÍRNIR SKÍRNIR (Journal of the Icelandic Literature Society),Copenhagen and Reykjavík, 1827-.

S.S. Sigfús Sigfússon, ÍSLENZKAR ÞJÓÐSÖGUR OG SAGNIR, 16 vols., Seyðisfjörður and Reykjavík, 1923-58.

V.Á. Valdimar Ásmundsson, ALÞINGISRÍMUR:1899-1901, Reykjavík, 1909.

INDEX OF TALE TYPES

INDEX OF TALE TYPES

Type numbers are from Antti Aarne and Stith Thompson, The Types of the Folktale, Helsinki, 1961. The rhymes which are included in this collection are similar, not identical, to the Aarne-Thompson tale types listed below.

Type No.   **Item No.**

IV. FORMULA TALES

Cumulative Tales

Type No.	Title	Item No.
2010A and B	The Twelve Days (Gifts) of Christmas	21
2015	The Goat Who Would Not Leave the Hazel Bush	22
2030	The Old Woman and Her Pig	22
2030B	Pulling the Needle Out of the Seamstress' Hand	22
2044	Pulling Up the Turnip	23, 24

Unfinished Tales

Type No.	Title	Item No.
2271	Mock Stories For Children	141, 142

LIST OF INFORMANTS
AND
THEIR CONTRIBUTIONS

LIST OF INFORMANTS AND THEIR CONTRIBUTIONS

Informants	Item No.
Anderson, Þórunn	126, 130
Bjarnason, Björn	107, 116, 117, 133, 139
Bjarnason, Ingibjörg	132
Bjarnason, Margrét	90
Bjarnason, Steinunn	15, 19
Bjarnason, Þórður	104
Björnsson, Sigríður	3, 4, 21, 22, 36, 40, 74, 91, 93, 94, 95, 96, 97, 98, 99, 101, 102, 105, 108, 110, 128
Björnsson, Þórey	26, 88
Böðvarsson, Tímoteus	119
Eiríksson, Herdís	24
Flanagan, Svava	67
Gillis, Gísli	65
Guðbjartsson, Andrés and Elísabet	47, 48
Helgason, Sigmundur	23, 78
Hjartarson, Hjörtur	87, 123
Holm, Gunnlaugur	7, 124, 143-285
Holm, Svanfríður	2, 7, 10, 92
Hornfjörð, Helgi	59
Howardson, Jón	25, 27, 72, 134

Informant	Story No.
Howardsson, Helga	106
Johnson, Dómhildur	62
Johnson, Valdimar	13, 16, 31, 34, 41, 42, 44, 45, 49, 50, 52, 63, 66, 69, 70, 79, 82, 127, 131, 136, 286-322
Johnson, Waldimar	32, 103
Jónsson, Gudmundur	58
Lyngdal, Friðfinnur	56, 80, 81
Magnússon, Gudrún	129
Mýrdal, Jón	5, 68, 77
Nordal, Lárus	33, 43, 46
Pálsson, Jón	9, 11, 12, 14
Pálsson, Guðrún	28, 140
Pálsson, Olga	64
Sigurðsson, Indíana	323-330
Simundson, Kár	100
Skúlason, Hrund	1, 29, 83, 84, 141, 142
Sveinsson, Sigurveig	6, 18, 20, 37, 38, 39, 51, 85, 86, 109, 111, 112
Sölvason, Jóhanna	30, 53, 73
Thorkelsson, Jóhanna	35, 54, 55, 57, 60, 61, 71, 75, 76, 89, 114, 118, 120, 135
Tómasson, Sigþóra	137
Valgarðsson, Steinunn	332
Vopnfjörð, Dagbjört	17

Map

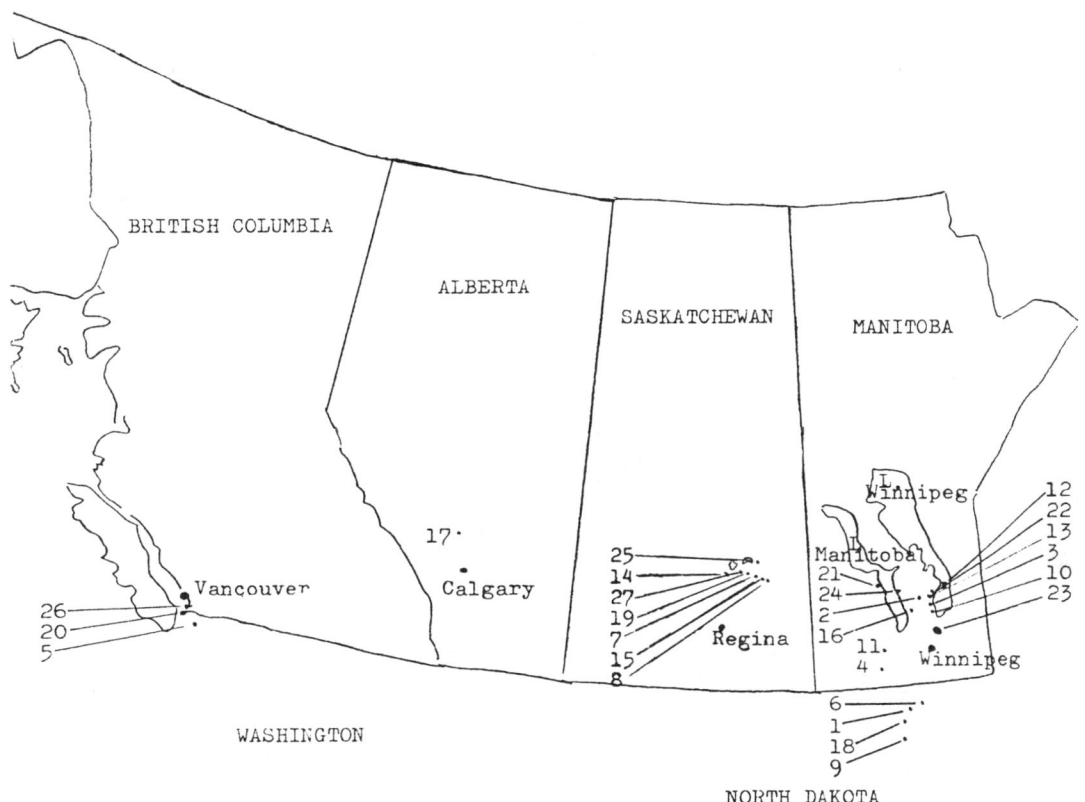

LOCATION OF SOME OF THE PLACES MENTIONED IN THIS COLLECTION

1 Akra
2 Arborg
3 Arnes
4 Baldur
5 Blaine
6 Cavalier
7 Elfros
8 Foam Lake
9 Gardar
10 Gimli
11 Glenboro
12 Hecla
13 Hnausa
14 Kandahar
15 Leslie
16 Lundar
17 Markerville
18 Mountain
19 Mozart
20 Point Roberts
21 Reykjavík
22 Riverton
23 Selkirk
24 Vogar
25 Wadena
26 White Rock
27 Wynyard